THE PERMANENT NOW

EXCEPTIONALLY ACCURATE GUIDANCE TO SPIRITUAL AWAKENING AND ENLIGHTENMENT, CRAFTED BY A LIVING BUDDHA

FRITZ

THE PERMANENT NOW

FIRST EDITION
SELF-PUBLISHED

Cover Design – FRITZ

ISBN 13: 978-0-9993800-8-6

Library of Congress Cataloging-in-Publication Data
FRITZ, T. Kevin
THE PERMANENT NOW: EXCEPTIONALLY ACCURATE GUIDANCE TO SPIRITUAL AWAKENING AND ENLIGHTENMENT, CRAFTED BY A LIVING BUDDHA / FRITZ
p. cm.
Spiritual life. I. Title.
2358132134

Your Most Accurate Self is Pure Awareness-Bliss The Permanent Now

CONTENTS

THE PERMANENT NOW

"Truth exists here and now."

Siddhartha Gautama

"Awareness isn't hidden. But you can only find it right now.
It's only now."

Bodhidharma

"Here it is – right now."

Huang Po

"Now is where Love breathes."

Rumi

INTRODUCTION

TIME

Then…

Time was everywhere

Time was a friend and an adversary

NOW…

Time is not real

It is integrative change in The Permanent Now

The Permanent Now provides exceptionally accurate guidance to spiritual Awakening and enlightenment, crafted by a living buddha - an Awaken.

Use The Permanent Now to broaden and deepen your internal self-Awareness and **literally Wake Up** in The Permanent Now and come to the direct experience and realization of The Permanent Now. Spiritually Awaken and unveil your most accurate Self is PURE AWARENESS-BLISS,

The Self, ALL, Nirvana, The Tao, THE SOURCE, Ultimate Union, Supreme Identity, Atman, Brahman, NOthing, etc. and your natural state of existence is enlightenment.

You unveil your most accurate Self and your natural state of existence by increasing the breadths and depths of your internal self-Awareness. A synergistic outcome of this increase in internal self-Awareness is the direct experience and realization Time is illusory and The Permanent Now is.

The Permanent Now guides you through, past and out of self-identification with and attachment to Time and all the illusions living in Time and into The Permanent Now.

Self-identification with and attachment to Time and all the illusions living in Time is resistance to The Permanent Now. Resisting manifested heaven creates illusory Time, Suffering and Fear, among other things.

Do not think, believe, accept and have faith the information in The Permanent Now is Reality.

Broaden and deepen your internal self-Awareness and unveil, through your direct experience and realization, your most accurate Self is THE SOURCE creating this universe*.

Do not give your authority away.

The only space/place there is, is Now. However, the thing you think you are is centered and rooted in the illusory reality/realm of past and future consciousness. The thing you think you are is not in Reality, The Permanent Now.

Self-identification with and attachment to Time and all the illusions living in Time completely blocks The Light of Awareness and The Permanent Now.

Stop self-identifying with, attaching to and myopically focusing on Time and the illusions living in Time. Stop sleeping in the illusory reality/realm of past and future consciousness and **literally Wake Up** in The Permanent Now.

Do not look for ways to become spiritually enlightened. You are, **already and of course**, ALL that you seek. You are, **already and of course**, spiritually enlightened*[2]. This is your natural state of existence. Congratulations, you have already made it. ☺

Unveil and come to the direct experience and realization of your natural state of existence. This unveiling happens in The Permanent Now. There is only this Moment, and this Moment integrates from within Itself. Time and the illusory reality/realm of past and future consciousness are in The Permanent Now, as is everything.

If you are not ready to dis-identify with and detach from Time, Fear, mental suffering, the thinker thinking the thoughts, the individual me/ego, etc., do not. This is fine. Acknowledge your move to apathy and enjoy your self-identification with and attachment to these illusions.

Before I Awakened, I thought, "I'll get all the information on spiritual enlightenment and then I'll be more informed and then I'll be better able to become spiritually enlightened." Awakening does not happen this way.

Read The Permanent Now with sincerity and attention. **Sincerity and attention are your guides.** By broadening and deepening your Awareness, The Permanent Now helps you dis-identify with and detach from the illusion of Time and all the illusions living in Time.

A constantly, consistently and continuously peaceful individual, culture, society and planet only happens when the individual human and the homo sapiens species Wakes Up and lives in Reality, The Permanent Now. Stop resisting The Permanent Now and end the individual, cultural, societal and planetary conflict and suffering.

NOTE

Your most accurate Self is not the individual me/ego inflated into what humans label god. Your most accurate Self is not a deity. Got it!? No superiority. No Relativeness.

Your most accurate Self is PURE AWARENESS-BLISS – THE SOURCE. ☺

NOTE2

You are born spiritually enlightened. Everything in this universe is innately spiritually enlightened. Ever since every human has been around twelve months old, all other humans (emphasizing parents, culture, society, etc.) teach you to self-identify with, attach to and accept their thoughts*[3]. This myopic self-identification with and myopic attachment to Time and all the illusions living in Time covers your innate and natural state of existence.

NOTE3

You unveil your most accurate Self "at the same place" **You** began veiling and covering up your most accurate Self. "This place" is Time.

humans teach thought and
Reality is not taught
unveil Awareness

DEFINITIONS

Full Acceptance

The cognitive ability to receive and hold on to What Is without mental creation, judgment or thought about What Is. An aspect of accurate Love

An Awaken

The label buddha is a Sanskrit pronoun and title meaning the Awakened one or the enlightened one.

An individual who has moved through, past and out of self-identification with and attachment to Time and all the illusions living in Time.

An individual who is absolutely Aware of PURE-AWARENESS-BLISS/THE SOURCE CREATING THIS UNIVERSE as your most accurate Self.

An individual who Wakes Up out of the illusion of Time.

An individual having direct experience and realization of The Permanent Now.

Awakening

Direct experience and realization of the resistance you give your inner self, lowering this resistance, hugging The Shadow and dis-identifying with and detaching from Time and all the illusions living in Time while increasing the constant, consistent and continuous breadth and depth of your internal self-Awareness

Aware and Awareness

Direct experience and realization

Being cognizant of and giving recognition to

Active Watching

Being

Your natural state of existence

Contemplation

Mental creation for The Permanent Now

Form

Any physical or mental creation

The Future

The illusory reality/realm of where human self-identity lives

Happiness

The mind's answer to what it thinks will give it peace

The Human Mind

The individual me/ego, the illusory thinker thinking the thoughts and <insert your name here>

Myopic human Awareness

Resistance to The Permanent Now

A tool which creates other tools

Illusions Living in Time

Self-identification with and attachment to; thought, mental cognition, the human mind, the individual me/ego, the thinker thinking the thoughts, the voice in your head, <insert your name here>, the reality/realm of past and future consciousness and mental suffering

Insanity

Doing the same thing over and over and over and expecting a different result, individually and as a species

INTEGRATION

The most fundamental, positive and one-way evolution of how this universe works. To integrate – verb – From this to that, with an additional synergistic variable added to that making that have added value and synergistic qualities compared to this. The evolution of physical life is one example of INTEGRATION.

Laugh out loud, with a positive attitude

The Permanent Now

Reality

The Eternal and always evolving current Moment

PURE AWARENESS-BLISS in motion

Manifested heaven

The Past

The illusory reality/realm of where human self-identity lives

Accurate Peace

An innate quality of **You** and an aspect of your most accurate Self

Problem

Anything taking your attention out of The Permanent Now.

An illusion

A thing living in the illusory reality/realm of past and future consciousness.

Reality

The Permanent Now

What Is before self-identification with and attachment to Time and all the illusions living in Time bends, filters, fades out and blocks The Permanent Now and What Is.

The Shadow

Resistance to all the unresolved aspects of your inner self. The part of your psyche which has no Awareness shining on it.

All your unresolved past and future issues you bury deep in the illusory reality/realm of past and future consciousness and use as resistance to The Permanent Now.

Spiritual Enlightenment

Your natural state of existence and no more suffering

Spirituality

Full acceptance of The Permanent Now

Suffering

Resisting The Permanent Now

Self-identification with and attachment to Time and all the illusions living in Time

Unconsciousness

Not fully being Here in The Permanent Now as Watching Awareness

Being human

Self-identification with and attachment to Time and all the illusions living in Time

You/Your most accurate Self

PURE AWARENESS-BLISS, The Self, Being, Spirit, ALL,

Stillness, NOthing, THE SOURCE CREATING THIS UNIVERSE, Ultimate Union, A Higher Power, Heaven and God in union, The Tao, Nirvana, Supreme Identity, Atman, Brahman, etc.

continuously
with a smile is the best way
this way, less folly

THE PERMANENT NOW'S WRITING STYLE

After literally Waking Up in The Permanent Now, I moved from Texas to the West Coast and for years sat on a bicycle, benches, beaches and then in forests and mountains and wrote down all the observations going through my Awareness and compiled these observations into a journal.

After new observations stop moving through my Awareness, I stopped compiling the journal. I organized the like-subject observations into CHAPTERS and now you have The Permanent Now.

The Permanent Now's sole purpose is increasing the breadth and depth of your internal self-Awareness. By eliciting an increase in the breadth and depth of your consistent internal self-Awareness, The Permanent Now's engaging and practical application writing style helps you literally Wake Up in The Permanent Now and come to the direct experience and realization of your most accurate Self. **Continuously with a smile. Do not stop. Do not expect.**

Every space, letter, word, sentence, paragraph, section and chapter in The Permanent Now are highly crafted and only signposts*. Signposts provide directions and therefore are maps of a territory; the realm of Awareness and the timeless, non-suffering Permanent Now*[2].

The presentation style or how a buddha crafts his/her signposts can be another potential catalyst for kick-starting your awakening.

The Permanent Now helps you understand spiritual enlightenment, which is labeled Awakening from now on, more accurately. Because you are, **already and of course**, spiritually enlightened, The Permanent Now helps awaken more Awareness from within you.

The Permanent Now exacerbates your persistence in folly in what can be a more expeditious and therefore an easier path toward the Inevitable. ☺

Your most accurate Self is ALL and NOthing. Your most accurate Self is this entire universe and PURE AWARENESS-BLISS – THE SOURCE creating this universe. ☺ This might sound wondrous, fantastical and maybe even a little unbelievable. Do not give your authority away. The Permanent Now's engaging and practical application writing style helps you come to your direct experience and realization of Awareness, The Permanent Now and your most accurate Self.

The Permanent Now does not go into great depth about how wonderful Waking Up and Awakening are. Because you are reading this, you have heard about spiritual enlightenment and how wonderful Awakening and spiritual enlightenment sound. Waking Up and Awakening are beyond words and mental comprehension.

LOGICAL SIMPLICITY

The Permanent Now shows you topics directly in front of your face and in observable Reality.

NULLIUS IN VERBA

Do not take my word for it. Come to your direct experience and realization of The Permanent Now. Do not give your authority away.

YOU ARE ALREADY SPIRITUALLY ENLIGHTENED

You cannot attain spiritual enlightenment. How can you attain That which **You**, **already and of course**, are? Self-identification with and attachment to Time and all the illusions living in Time block your direct experience and realization of your natural state of Being and The Permanent Now.

PERSISTENCE IN FOLLY

There is nothing you can do to Awaken. Because you self-identify with and attach to Time, the mind and its doings, you think you must do something. This perspective is understandable. All you know is doing. Ever since you were around twelve months old, you have no direct experience and realization of what non-doing and Being is. Non-doing and Being live in The Permanent Now.

You self-identify with and attach to a thing living in the illusory reality/realm of past and future consciousness. The Permanent Now helps you burn up your unnecessary desire for doings, so when you tire and there are no doings left, the only thing left is Being and Laughter because you tried so hard to do nothing. Stop doing and give sincerity and attention to increasing the breadth and depth of your internal self-Awareness. Doing lives in Time. Being lives in The Permanent Now.

HOW CAN THIS BE EXPEDITIOUS?

The Permanent Now helps expedite your Persistence in Folly so you do not run around like a chicken with its head cut off, like I did, bumping into obstacles, as I did, and do doings, which need not be done, like I did, repeatedly, as I did*[3]. ☺

THE INEVITABLE?

The Inevitable is unveiling your most accurate Self, and it is always happening in The Permanent Now.

NESS

The suffix NESS is frequently used in The Permanent Now. Words are labels used to represent direct experiences and realizations. The suffix NESS is a label pointing to a direct experience and realization.

The word SMOOTH is a signpost pointing to and describing the quality of a thing. The quality of the surface of a well-polished mirror is its smoothness. When touching a well-polished mirror's surface, you come to the direct experience and realization of what the word SMOOTHNESS is pointing. The ness of smooth is that which is being experienced and directly realized through your level of Awareness when touching a thing.

***

Come to the direct experience and realization of the topics brought up in The Permanent Now and become more Aware of more things and unveil the Awareness before, during and after all things. Increase your ability to Awaken by unveiling Awareness, which is the Within Ness and Behind Ness of everything. The Permanent Now does not ask you to do, think or believe anything. It helps you unveil the Awareness within you and within and behind the only

Moment of LIFE there is. The only Moment you are ever in. The only Moment you are ever Aware of. This Moment integrates from within Itself*4.

NOTE

A paraphrased Zen saying states, "Don't look at my finger. Look at where my finger points." More accurately, move through, past and out of self-identification with and attachment to Time and all the illusions living in Time and unveil the ETERNAL and INFINITE field of Watching Awareness.

NOTE2

More on this in Chapter Five.

NOTE3

More on this in Chapter Six.

NOTE4

More on this in Chapters Seventeen, Nineteen and Twenty-One.

for guidance, sometimes
the sword's better than smiling
pro transparency!

ACCURATE GUIDANCE

You do not need a master, guru or
guide to help you with your spiritual Awakening.

You need accurate guidance, sincerity and attention.

You are the only one responsible for your awakening. Apply sincerity and attention to the guidance not the buddha. Buddhas come and go. For over fifty centuries, Awakens have been coming and going in every culture. Guidance is Permanence is Watching Awareness.

Do not apply attention and devotion to the buddha. It is the buddha's responsibility to apply her/his sincerity, attention and devotion to the accuracy of the guidance.

ACCURATE GUIDANCE

A buddha who has already accomplished what you are looking to accomplish can only give accurate guidance. Do not seek human guidance. Humans cannot provide accurate guidance. A person inside the illusions of Time, Suffering, past and future consciousness and the individual me/ego cannot provide accurate guidance out of these illusions. How can they??? How can a person guide another person out of something they are not out of themselves???

Humans teach humans how to think and how to think differently. Thinking differently does not get you out of the illusions of Time, Suffering, past and future consciousness and the individual me/ego. Thinking differently is like providing a painkiller for your illusory suffering. The suffering is still there; humans mask it. Watch religious and secular thought leaders*. Can you fly by pulling up your bootstraps?

Buddhas are the only authors Aware of what we are talking about. Outside an Awaken's guidance, all other writings are a degraded and out-of-focus copy of an original and most likely complete inaccuracy. Find originals.

All you need is to constantly give attention to Reality and whatever might enter it for the rest of your life, pssst – guess what! ☺, dis-identify with and detach from Time and all the illusions living in Time, come to the direct experience and realization of the resistance to aspects of your inner self you do not want to deal with, lower this internal resistance by watching everything, fully accept those aspects of your inner self, be Aware of the mind and therefore no longer self-identify with and attach to the illusion you are the thinker thinking the thoughts, come to the direct experience and realization of the answer to the question, **Who am I?,** unveil the simplest of facts that Time is illusory and literally Wake Up at least once and preferably twice. ☺ ☺

THEORETICAL CONVERSATION AND PRACTICAL APPLICATION WRITING STYLES

When choosing accurate guidance, find a buddha who delivers the information about how to literally Wake Up in The Permanent Now, spiritually Awaken, dis-identify with and detach from Time and all the illusions living in Time and how to come to the direct experience and realization of your most accurate Self through a practical application writing style rather than a theoretical conversation writing style.

The Permanent Now's practical application writing style guides you through, past and out of self-identification with and attachment to Time and all the illusions living in Time and into Awareness, spiritual Awakening and The Permanent Now.

The theoretical conversation writing style keeps your myopic Awareness self-identifying with and attaching to Time and all the illusions living in Time.

Two examples showing some differences between the theoretical conversation writing style and the practical application writing style are learning how to fly and learning how to ride a bicycle. Use these as parallels for Awakening.

THEORETICAL CONVERSATION WRITING STYLE

Paralleling the theoretical conversation writing style with the flying example is, "When you learn how to fly, the wind will feel so wonderful moving across your face. When flying through a cloud, moisture will take on an entirely new dimension. If you are afraid of heights and you learn how to fly high, when you are up in the sky eating that pie and looking down toward the ground, you will laugh and giggle and give your nose a little wiggle!"

Paralleling the theoretical conversation writing style with the riding a bicycle example is, "The bicycle has two wonderful wheels. It has humongous handlebars. It has a splendorous seat. It has a fantastic frame and pleasant pedals. It feels so wonderful to ride a bike. Etc."

The theoretical conversation writing style basks in the glory of mental cognition, thought and information and keeps your myopic Awareness focused on mental cognition, thought and information. This writing style is mental masturbation. Do you want to mentally masturbate or spiritually Awaken, unveil The Permanent Now and come to the direct experience and realization of your most accurate Self?

The Tao Te Ching and most works written by buddhas have the theoretical conversation writing style. If you want to read about the subject of spiritual Awakening and enlightenment, the Tao Te Ching and most other writings crafted by buddhas are great literary works. This writing style does not actively engage you to spiritually Awaken, unveil The Permanent Now and your most accurate Self and come to the direct experience and realization of your natural state of existence.

Many Awakens become cartographers not deliverers of accurate guidance.

Learning and understanding about spiritual Awakening and enlightenment is not the same as understanding how to let go and drop self-identification with and attachment to Time and all the illusions living in Time and through direct experience and realization Wake Up in The Permanent Now, spiritually Awaken and unveil Awareness, your most accurate Self and PURE AWARENESS-BLISS.

Paralleling The Permanent Now's practical application writing style with these two examples, The Permanent Now is a guidebook providing exceptionally accurate guidance on how to fly and how to ride a bicycle.

Practical Application Writing Style

Paralleling The Permanent Now's practical application writing style with the flying example is, "The first step in flying is Step X. Here is Step X. After you master Step X, move to Step Y and eventually Step Z. During Step X, you might have an issue with (insert challenge here). The way through this challenge is (insert action here). Practice with these exercises. Do not stop. Do not expect. All the best."

Paralleling The Permanent Now's practical application writing style with the riding a bicycle example is, "Sit on the seat, grab the handlebars, put one foot on a pedal, give yourself a push with your other foot, put that foot on the other pedal and while balancing, start pedaling. After you fall over, get up with a smile, get back on the bicycle and repeat. All the best."

When crafted by a buddha, the practical application writing style can broaden and deepen your myopic Awareness through, past and out of self-identification with and attachment to Time and all the illusions living in Time and into Awareness, Awakening and The Permanent Now.

When crafted by a buddha, the practical application writing style provides accurate guidance. The theoretical conversation writing style is mental masturbation. Reading Awakens' personal accounts will not help you Awaken.

NON-SUFFERING LIFE FORMS CAN HELP HUMANS

There are many wonderful life forms on Earth and they can all provide accurate guidance to humans. Watch Nature. By illuminating things, Nature can help you with your awakening. Dogs are one such opportunity. Dogs live in The Permanent Now and with humans. Dogs are wonderful signposts to The Permanent Now and no more suffering.

Another life form, which has transcended and let go of Time and all the illusions living in Time, is an Awaken. Some buddhas communicate more accurately than other buddhas. If I was still searching, I would find an Awaken who Woke Up twice and the second time was ABSOLUTE.

The first time a sleeping buddha Wakes Up is when (s)he Wakes Up in The Permanent Now and comes to the direct experience and realization that self-identification with and attachment to Time and all the illusions living in Time is illusory.

The second time a buddha Wakes Up is when (s)he Wakes Up out of the dream you and I call this universe and Wakes Up into; **REAL LIFE**, PURE AWARENESS-BLISS, your most accurate Self, THE SOURCE creating this universe, ABSOLUTE NOthingness and comes to the direct experience and realization this entire universe is a dream of motion and INTEGRATION by your most accurate Self.

Buddhas at this breadth and depth of Awareness are generally accurate communicators.

TRIANGULATING GUIDANCE

Triangulating guidance increases its overall accuracy. The Permanent Now triangulates its guidance using these three bearings; the outer physical world and your five senses, your inner world and your psyche and showing how one of the three fundamental pillars of this universe, Time, is an illusion. Use these three bearings to more accurately spiritually Awaken and unveil The Permanent Now and your most accurate Self and live your most accurate life.

NOTE

Except for skill-based guidance, religious and secular thought leaders teach humans to self-identify with and attach to this thought over that thought. Relativeness.

They talk about and teach ideas, thoughts and knowledge. They expound, "If you think good thoughts, you will have good thoughts running around in your mind and therefore be a good person and have a good life. If you think bad thoughts, you will have bad thoughts running around in your mind and therefore be a bad person and have a bad life."

Self-identifying with, attaching to and following their teachings keeps your myopic Awareness self-identified with and attached to the individual me/ego and keeps you in Time, Suffering and Fear, among other things. Religious and secular thought leaders hypnotize humans and are the hypnotizers of humanity. This is an extremely accurate human behavior and not accurate if you want to unveil The Permanent Now, your most accurate Self, spiritually Awaken and let go of your mental suffering.

Religious and secular thought leaders do not explain how to spiritually Awaken, how to come to the direct experience and realization of The Permanent Now and how to unveil your most accurate Self. How could they??? They live in Time and the illusory reality/realm of past and future consciousness.

If you want to spiritually Awaken, unveil The Permanent Now and your most accurate Self and let go of Time, Suffering and Fear, among other things, religious and secular thought leaders' proselytizing wastes your time. Religious and secular thought leaders are the monkey in the following analogy.

THE MONKEY AND FISH ANALOGY

Once upon a time, a vain, self-righteous and well-intentioned monkey bent down and took a fish out of a stream and put the fish up in a tree. Thinking he was doing good, the monkey proudly exclaimed,

> "Here, let me help you! You will drown in that water! We live in trees, not water*[2]!"

After you Wake Up, you come to the direct experience and realization this entire universe is already being taken care of by your most accurate Self. When you resist The Permanent Now, you disrupt The Flow of the universe and you muddy up the water. Let go of the illusory control over your illusory self and others and show the universe you have the control. Let the water settle.

NOTE2

Watch human behavior. This human behavior has been happening ever since humans myopically self-identified with and attached to Time and the illusory thinker thinking the thoughts and accepted The Illusion of Separation.

Until you stop resisting The Permanent Now and come to direct experience and realization of your most accurate Self, this "I know more than you…" mentality will continue. Humans have good intentions*[3].

NOTE3

The path to hell is paved with good intentions. Stop running around and obsessing on making good thoughts overcome and overpower bad thoughts.

go beyond signposts
by increasing Awareness
Watch and unveil You

traveling beyond
conceptualization
signposts point past thought

SIGNPOSTS

Do not mistake the accuracy of a signpost
with the actuality of Being

Every space, letter, word, sentence, paragraph, section and chapter in The Permanent Now are highly crafted and only signposts. Signposts provide guidance to a territory; the realm of PURE AWARENESS-BLISS, the timeless, non-suffering Permanent Now and accurate Reality.

Signposts are pointers representing direct experience and realization. Signposts broaden and deepen the level of consistent internal self-Awareness you already have, which can help you Awaken. Signposts provide guidance so you can move through, past and out of self-identification with and attachment to Time and thought consciousness and unveil Watching Awareness, which lives in The Permanent Now.

Use The Permanent Now to expedite and simplify your awakening by understanding signposts and Be where they point. When you look at a map and you are mentally digesting the information, representations and symbols, you are not in the territory the map represents. Direct experience, realization, Awareness and The Permanent Now are the territory for spiritual Awakening. A buddha's communications are maps and directions for you to use and guide yourself into direct experience and realization of Awareness and The Permanent Now. Awakens craft visual and auditory maps and directions, which provide guidance to Awakening.

Ultimately, every question asked about a signpost is an instrument used to wrap up signposts into the conceptualization stage. Can you see the cyclical nature of the mind? Signposts should not be conceptualized and thought about, only.

Signposts are not about how to get to Here and The Permanent Now with thought and by using thought.

CONCEPTUALIZATION

Initially, understanding signposts through conceptualization is needed. Obviously, you need to understand the subject, verb and predicate of the sentence and how the signpost is pointing you to Being. Thinking in more detail, better than someone else, more exquisitely than you used to and "more deeply" will never get you to unveil The Permanent Now. You must broaden and deepen your self-Awareness and come to the direct experience and realization of The Permanent Now. After conceptualizing the information, no additional amount of knowledge or learning can help you Awaken.

Do not judge signposts. Judging keeps you in Relativeness and keeps **You** self-identifying with and attaching to Time, all the illusions living in Time and in the conceptualization stage, which is Step Zero. This judging by the human mind is cyclical. <u>The mind is very cyclical</u>. Watch for the cyclical nature of the human mind.

A signpost shows you a way beyond it. Beyond a conceptualized signpost is Watching Awareness, The Permanent Now and Being. Ninety-nine point nine plus percent of humans stay in the reality/realm of conceptualization. Books written about spirituality from human authors are written while in the reality/realm of conceptualization, thought and mental activity and not from direct experience and realization of Awareness and in The Permanent Now.

A buddha's task is crafting accurate signposts*. An accurate signpost ignites Awareness to shine from within and can be the beginnings of awakening and unveiling Awareness. A buddha's craft is creating a signpost that increases the breadth and depth of your internal self-Awareness.

Understanding a signpost, or what a signpost represents, allows you to describe the signpost. Awakening is not the understanding of signposts, only. Understanding the complexities of the signpost helps you more accurately see where the signpost is pointing. Everyone likes a well-detailed map. Awakening does not happen to the human who can recite, recreate or rehash signposts. Awakening happens where the signpost points. Awakening happens when you proverbially walk past the signpost, drop self-identification with and attachment to Time and thought consciousness and unveil Watching Awareness, The Permanent Now and your natural state of existence.

After listening to me speak about signposts, a gentleman conceptualized, organized and wrapped all the signposts in The Permanent Now into a nice, neat and organized mental box. He put a mental bow on the mental box and put the mental box on a mental shelf in his mind. He still suffers.

When signposts are conceptualized, organized and wrapped into a nice, neat and mentally conceptualized box, the human mind is creating another signpost pointing back to the original signpost. Pretty cyclical, huh?

When the mind creates another signpost pointing back to the original signpost, the mind feels good because it thinks it has done what it needs to do. The mind has done all it can. The mind conceptualizes, organizes and labels what it encounters. The mind does not understand Being.

Conceptualization is needed. The mind thinks after the conceptualization stage is complete the process is over. When the mind thinks this, the human always falls short of Awakening. After conceptualization has occurred, you are ready to drop self-identification with and attachment to Time and thought consciousness and begin unveiling and integrating Watching Awareness. The conceptualization stage is Step Zero in increasing the breadth and depth of your consistent internal self-Awareness, not the final step.

OVER FIFTY CENTURIES OF REPETITION

As with all Form, signposts have structure and content. The content of a signpost has changed a little because of linguistic- and cultural-based issues with how signposts are crafted today relative to the last fifty-plus centuries.

Does this grab your sincerity and attention? How can something, which has been going on for over fifty centuries have the same message while the time, culture, society, etc. have a little effect on the message, all the while having the same message for over five millennia?

Has this ever happened with anything else in the history of this entire planet? Have you ever played The Message Game in elementary school? One session with over two players produces inaccurate outcomes from the initial saying.

Find another situation where the same message is being delivered for over five millennia and the only differences in the message are linguistic- and cultural-based differences of the specific messenger because of their time in the last fifty-plus centuries. How can this be?

Reality is Reality. Awakens cannot change Reality or What Is. If you drop a rock on your head a million years ago or a million years from now, the rock will always hurt. You cannot change the reality of your head hurting when a rock is dropped on your head. Does this make this topic more attentive? Awakens point you toward Reality. Awakens cannot change Reality. We provide guidance to help you guide yourself to COME BACK TO NOW, Wake Up and come to the direct experience and realization of Watching Awareness, The Permanent Now and your most accurate Self.

Describing the intricacies of a signpost, how interesting it is, how it makes you feel, etc., creates reflexive thought about the signpost. You made another signpost pointing to the signpost you think you are Aware of. This cyclical thought process might make you the star of a dinner party. It does not stop your suffering. It is the suffering.

At this point of understanding, you can adequately talk about the signpost, and you are not where you need to Be to begin your awakening. Being is not a location. Being is a broader and deeper state of Awareness. Be in the timeless Permanent Now and signposts are no longer necessary.

THE DIFFERENCE

Signposts do not ask you to do something, think a certain way, hold certain beliefs, values, emotions and feelings. This is what humans ask other humans to do.

Signposts guide you to drop self-identification with and attachment to Time and all the illusions living in Time and through direct experience and realization unveil Watching Awareness, The Permanent Now, your most accurate Self and your natural state of existence.

NOTE

Buddhas-of-long-a-go's guidance was labeled signposts, as well. Two millennia ago, a person making actual signposts made signposts out of wood. Two millennia ago, a person working with wood was known as a carpenter. There are only different versions of your most accurate Self.

resisting Heaven
creates the search for pleasure
breathe deep and Watching

I used to search for
acceptance in outer things
The Permanent Now

FRITZ'S GAME OF HIDE AND SEEK

At its most fundamental level, the entire human species is searching for a way into Happiness and Connection or searching for a way out of Suffering and into Connection. This searching is the Game of Hide and Seek. The following is a simplification of Fritz's Game of Hide and Seek.

This life is not better or worse, and not filled with more or less Grace than any other life.

I began focusing on my mind as who I was around second grade, from six to seven, when I accepted mentally talking to myself as normal. Thus, for most of my life, I was deeply entrenched in my mind and so deeply identified with things I created, which were ninety-nine plus percent living in the illusory reality/realm of future consciousness.

Around fifteen, I began feeling and sensing an increasing drive to get out of an increasing level of mental suffering I felt from within. I was Aware of my mental suffering and most importantly I was Aware I wanted to find a way out of my mental suffering. I did not want to hold on to it like a badge of honor, the way I witnessed so many humans do or deny the reality of having mental suffering, which everyone else did. I never understood why mental suffering was a thing.

This is when I started The Search to end my mental suffering out there in another and an other. I constantly looked for Happiness and Connection in another and an other. I tried to get out of mental suffering by doing.

In no particular order of importance, some of my outward doings were; at twelve I began working seven days a week delivering newspapers, at fourteen I quit my paper route and forged my birth certificate so I could "grow up" by working at a national fast-food hamburger chain, the next summer I took summer school to advance into another honors class in high school, two broken arms, three entrepreneurial ventures, the search for positive relationships, approval from people I admired, a top degree from a top university, a lot of nicotine, a lot of work, a lot of alcohol, promotions with increasing responsibility, marriage, two entrepreneurial ventures, chasing money, clinically diagnosed depression, divorce, I was a student and instructor for Dale Carnegie™ and Outward Bound™ and an instructor for Broadreach™, I went on hundreds of first dates, I read dozens and dozens of sales and self-help books and books aimed at Spirituality written by humans, I developed a lot of hobbies, I climbed two, fourteen-thousand foot plus peak mountains in the Colorado Rockies, I lived in fourteen homes in the twenty years after college, sailing to a different continent, personal bankruptcy for financially supporting a family member after their medical crisis and throughout my life I felt a certain perceived control over mental suffering when I became effective and efficient in the skill and art of helping people laugh.

Some of my inward doings were; one of my top three internal life priorities was to keep an open heart throughout; break-ups, divorce, endings of friendships, the passing of pets and loved ones, several broken hearts, etc. I did not want those experiences to change, bend or break my personality the way I witnessed this happen in others. I golden shadowed every relationship I had. From around seven until thirty-five, I spent thirty minutes to an hour every night while in bed examining my day's actions. Through-out my twenties and thirties, I spoke with psychologists about my feelings and current life-situation. When people snubbed me personally and professionally, I was Aware it was about their internal issues, not my outward behavior. I consciously never went into my ego to "get over" on someone to make me feel better, bigger or more important. I consciously never went into Relativeness within the social dynamics I had with business and social acquaintances, friends and loved ones.

At thirty-seven, a doctor diagnosed my body with ulcerative colitis and told me it was probably because of stress. ☺ At thirty-eight, I was going crazy, if not already. I was not going out of my mind. I was going deep into my mind. More accurately, my myopic Awareness was becoming more myopic.

I could not keep juggling all the balls and keep all the plates spinning. A month before my thirty-ninth birthday, I was in my office preparing for a client-conference call and an indescribably intense and comforting experience begins.

I start peacefully crying, and I look up from the desk. Every object in the room is oozing light. I look at the carpet and carpet-colored light is oozing up and out of the carpet. I look at the office walls and wall-colored light is oozing sideways out of the walls. I look at the desk, the computer and everything else in the office and light is oozing out of those objects, as well. I look outside the office and the carpet, walls and ceiling are oozing carpet-, wall- and ceiling-colored light. I check my focus level, again. I stand up, leave the office and look down the hall. Everything is oozing brilliant light!

The Light's brilliance is indescribable. I can only accurately describe the experience as ACCURATE PEACE. These words and signposts do not and cannot accurately describe.

I walk back into the office, sit back down in the chair and continue peacefully crying.

My mind is out of fuel. Like a star running too hot and too long, my mind cracks, implodes and then explodes open like a star exploding into a type 1a supernova.

BANG!

While looking up, my Awareness and Existence Itself increases in **CLARITY** and **ACCURACY***.

I bend forward while my knees and legs move up to my chest. While watching the ceiling, I watch and feel myself take a deep breath and then, EXHALING. **I Wake Up in The Permanent Now.** The Light of Awareness is shining in The Permanent Now. **Awareness Is All There Is***2.

What remains is PURE AWARENESS and a level of BEING, PEACE and STILLNESS so very stable and so very deep; labels, words, sounds and conceptualization can never accurately describe PURE AWARENESS. ☺!! ☺!!

With this transitioning and integration, I come to the direct experience and realization…

THERE ARE NO PROBLEMS NOW

THIS ENTIRE UNIVERSE IS MANIFESTED
PURE AWARENESS-BLISS

ALL IS FORGIVEN

There is no real individual me. The individual me/ego is not in Reality. I am not what I thought I was! ☺! The individual thinker thinking the thoughts is an illusion existing in the illusory reality/realm of past and future consciousness. You are not the individual mind, person or identity you call <insert your name here>. Stop self-identifying with and giving myopic attachment to the illusions and end Time, Suffering and Fear, among other things.

During the next several years, I had a lot of brightenings. Many were long, strong, rich, deep and highly accurate. In two brightenings, the division between the subject of the situation, what humans call themselves, and all the objects of the situation, what humans call everything outside themselves went away. **There is only Awareness.** There is only This. ☺! ☺! Twice more. Again. **Total fun!** ☺! ☺!

The following Happening is a broader breadth of CLARITY and a deeper depth of ACCURACY to spiritual Awakening, coming to the direct experience and realization of your most accurate Self and PURE AWARENESS-BLISS. Nine months after I Woke Up and unveiled The Permanent Now, I simply, gently and spontaneously came to an ABSOLUTE non-resistance to everything.

I Woke Up again. My Awareness left the relative reality of this universe and integrated back into ABSOLUTE REALITY. I came to the direct experience and realization of; your most accurate Self, THE SOURCE creating this universe, ALL, ABSOLUTE NOTHING NESS, what REAL LIFE is and PURE AWARENESS-BLISS.

PERMANENCE CLARITY ACCURACY

With this transitioning and integration, I come to the direct experience and realization…

THIS UNIVERSE IS A DREAMING

This universe is not absolutely real. This universe is only relatively real. Your most accurate Self, PURE AWARENESS-BLISS, is creating an Experience or a Dream of Motion and Integrative Change, which we call this universe. **Literally.**

REAL LIFE IS ABSOLUTE REALITY is your most accurate Self is PURE AWARENESS-BLISS IS REAL LIFE. **Y**ou are THE SOURCE creat<u>ing</u> this universe. Your most accurate Self is the Awareness within and behind the constant, consistent and continuous creat<u>ing</u> of everything in this universe. In REAL LIFE, **Y**ou are Aware of **Y**ourself and the dynamic of The Present Moment*[3]. **Y**ou are Aware of everything. **SHEER EXUBERANCE!** The above just happened. I did not do anything because there is no individual me to do it.

ABSOLUTE non-resistance to ALL or what humans call "death" is a transitioning back to; REAL LIFE, PURE AWARENESS-BLISS, NOthing, THE SOURCE and your most accurate Self. <u>Existence does not end when you die</u>. **Y**ou go back being PURE AWARENESS-BLISS and Existence Itself. **Y**ou Wake Up from the dream you and I call this universe. **<u>Motion ends and your most accurate Self is</u>.** <u>Death is of the mind</u>. <u>Your most accurate Self does not die</u>. Only the illusory self-identification with and attachment to Time and all the illusions living in Time end and then The Dream you and I call this universe ends.

Your most accurate Self in motion is the entire universe. What you can see, touch, smell, hear and taste is Awareness in Integrative Change. **Y**ou are ALL. **Y**ou are THE SOURCE. Every form you see in this entire universe is a different version of your most accurate Self.

The Search is not out there in another and an other. <u>The Search is unveiling The Permanent Now</u>*4.

WHAT IS REAL?

This universe is a Dream of Motion and INTEGRATION by your most accurate Self*5. SPACE, TIME and FORM are variables creating the ability for Motion and integrative change to exist. Nothing in this universe is permanent. Motion and the opportunity for Motion to exist elsewhere is what Change is. SPACE, TIME and FORM began almost fourteen billion years ago and therefore will end. This universe is an expanding bubble of Integrative Change encapsulated within absolutely NOthing, PURE AWARENESS-BLISS and your most accurate Self. This entire universe is within **Y**ou.

Your most accurate Self is timeless and timelessness. Now has no beginning or end. It is always Now. Now is always here. Unveil Eternity in the Present Moment. Eternity is The Permanent Now.

Eternity is not the continuation of the future forever and ever, amen. ☺ Eternity is Permanence is Non-change is ABSOLUTELY REAL is Eternity. Your most accurate Self is the only thing which never changes. NOthing does not change. Non-motion does not change. Stillness never changes. PURE AWARENESS accepts ALL and therefore reflects ALL. PURE AWARENESS does not hold on to and therefore is never conditioned or changed.

The only thing Real and Permanent in this universe is the only thing existing in and is permanent in all three areas of consciousness; awake, dream and deep sleep. The only thing existing in and permanent in all three areas of consciousness and It is not "a thing," is Awareness. **Total fun!** ☺! ☺! An aspect of your most accurate Self is PURE POTENTIALITY. Are you interested in unveiling and uncovering these simple facts through your direct experience and realization?

Through repetition, you must COME BACK TO NOW, stay Here, Now, literally Wake Up and unveil The Permanent Now and then literally Wake Up again and unveil your most accurate Self, PURE AWARENESS-BLISS.

NOTE

Imagine driving your car in an extremely rainy downpour for your entire life while your car windshield constantly collects your entire life's rain and debris and the windshield wipers are not on.

Now, imagine the windshield wipers instantly turning on and instantly clearing away all the rain and debris which has been hitting and collecting on your car windshield for as long as you can remember. CLARITY.

While this is happening, picture Existence Itself rotating counterclockwise approximately twenty percent. ACCURACY.

NOTE2

<u>There are no real edges, barriers or divisions in this universe</u>. The thing we all call Space is not nothingness between things. Everything in this universe is a different hue of PURE AWARENESS-BLISS. **<u>There is only PURE AWARENESS-BLISS.</u>**

NOTE3

Your most accurate Self does not remember, so be in Joy in this life.

NOTE4

The Search is not "a search." It is increasing the breadth and depth of your internal self-Awareness. This increase in the breadth and depth of your Watching Awareness can increase your potentiality to literally Wake Up and unveil accurate Reality, The Permanent Now.

NOTE5

This entire universe and everything in it on both the Newtonian and atomic scales is eventually Integrative Change. The Dream of Integration began almost fourteen billion years ago and The Dream will end trillions upon trillions of years from now and always in The Permanent Now.

That is a short dream. ☺

immortality
Gilgamesh's quest is done
The Permanent Now

search for Holy Grail
Galahad's search is over
The Permanent Now

THE GAME OF HIDE AND SEEK

At its most fundamental level, the entire human species is searching for a way into Happiness and Connection or searching for a way out of Suffering and into Connection. This searching is The Game of Hide and Seek.

Humans are unAware of The Game of Hide and Seek for what it is. The search for Happiness and Connection is so embedded and ingrained within the fabric of what humans call daily life The Game continues for everyone, except for those who literally Wake Up.

THE HUMAN CONDITION

Humans are searching for Happiness and Connection within something out there in another and an other. The mind's reality is this universe or of Space, Time and Form.

The mind thinks it can find lasting Happiness and Connection in the things it knows. It cannot. It has been trying for over two-hundred thousand years and in over one hundred and eight billion different lifetimes. It never has and never will find lasting Happiness and Connection. Read the definition of Insanity, right now. Outside using the mind as the tool which creates other tools, the mind is resistance to The Permanent Now. When there is resistance to The Permanent Now, conflict arises and suffering is close behind.

THE SEEKER

You are the Seeker and the Hider is Happiness and Connection. The mind thinks it will find what it is searching for in another and an other; Space, Time and Form. It does for a short while until there is more resistance, which is self-identification with and attachment to Time and all the illusions living in Time. Your myopic Awareness goes back and self-identifies with and attaches to another and an other Space, Time and Form.

The Game of Hide and Seek is suffering. Self-identification with and attachment to temporal movement out of The Permanent Now is suffering. Self-identification with and attachment to the illusory past or future consciousness is suffering. What humans call "my life" is The Game of Hide and Seek and suffering.

PHYSICAL FORM

You search for Happiness and Connection, the mind's answer to accurate Peace, in physical Form. Humans search for Happiness and Connection in; money, sex, houses, cars, clothes, jewelry, food, alcohol, sugar, caffeine, nicotine and other drugs, entertainment, tools, etc. Happiness and Connection are there until they are not. **Happiness and Connection with physical Form do not last. Illusions do not last.** Conflict arises and suffering is close behind. After you get frustrated enough and become Aware of a desire to leave suffering behind, you might stop searching for what you think Happiness and Connection are in physical Form.

Now, you understand and might realize you cannot find what you think Happiness and Connection are in physical Form. The mind thinks it can find lasting Happiness and Connection in physical Form or things. It cannot. It has been trying for over two-hundred thousand years and in over one hundred and eight billion different lifetimes. It never has and never will.

The search continues…

SPACE

You search for Happiness and Connection, the mind's answer to accurate Peace, in Space. You search in Space or different locations – vacations, a better life in another location, etc. You go to those locations and the mind finds Happiness and Connection in another and an other location. Happiness and Connection are there until they are not. **Happiness and Connection with Space do not last. Illusions do not last.** Conflict arises and suffering is close behind. After you get frustrated enough and become Aware of a desire to leave suffering behind, you might stop searching for what you think Happiness and Connection are in Space or locations. Do not go on an expedition to Nepal, Tibet, Mecca or any other place believing you will come closer to spiritual Awakening. Location means nothing.

Now, you understand and might realize you cannot find what you think Happiness and Connection are in Space. The mind thinks it can find lasting Happiness and Connection in Space or locations. It cannot. It has been trying for over two-hundred thousand years and in over one hundred and eight billion different lifetimes. It never has and never will.

The search continues…

TIME

You search for Happiness and Connection, the mind's answer to accurate Peace, in Time. You might understand and realize Happiness and Connection with normal time does not work. Therefore, you create and look for

Happiness and Connection in special time and celebration times. Happiness and Connection are there until they are not. **Happiness and Connection with Time do not last. Illusions do not last.** Conflict arises and suffering is close behind. After you get frustrated enough and Aware of a desire to leave suffering behind, you might stop searching for what you think Happiness and Connection are in Time and time-identification*.

Now, you understand and might realize you cannot find what you think lasting Happiness and Connection are in Time. The mind thinks it can find lasting Happiness and Connection in Time. It cannot. It has been trying for over two-hundred thousand years and in over one hundred and eight billion different lifetimes. It never has and never will.

The search continues…

MENTAL FORM

You search for Happiness and Connection, the mind's answer to accurate Peace, in mental Form. The only thing left in this universe to search in, from the mind's perspective, is mental Form*[2]. You search for Happiness and Connection in the mental relationships you have with; your spouse, significant other, friends, colleagues, children, group, culture and society, etc. Happiness and Connection are there until they are not. **Happiness and Connection with mental Form do not last. Illusions do not last.**

Conflict arises and suffering is close behind. After you get frustrated enough and become Aware of a desire to leave suffering behind, you might stop searching for what you think Happiness and Connection are in mental Form or Thought-identification.

The search continues…

The last step and the only <u>perceived</u> way out of this challenge is creating the style or classification of thought labeled religion. <u>Religion is a style of thought or a classification of mental activity</u>. This style of thought is the holy grail of thought. Pun intended. ☺ Religion is the style of thought, which bested all other thoughts/mental activity in the search for what the mind thinks Happiness and Connection are. This classification or style of thought is the perfect thought of Space, the perfect thought of Time and the perfect thought of Form. Thought-heaven. Happiness and Connection are there until they are not. **Happiness and Connection with religious mental Form do not last. Illusions do not last.** Watch religion. Conflict arises and suffering is close behind. After you get frustrated enough and become Aware of a desire to leave suffering behind, you might stop searching for what you think Happiness and Connection are in religious mental Form.

Now, you understand and might realize you cannot find what you think Happiness and Connection are in any type of mental Form. The mind thinks it can find lasting Happiness and Connection in mental things. It cannot. It has been trying for over two-hundred thousand years and in over one hundred and eight billion different lifetimes. It never has and never will.

The search continues…

LET GO

Let go of the search for Happiness and Connection in Space, Time and Form and Be in the present Moment*[3]. COME BACK TO NOW. With repetition stay Here, Now, come to the direct experience and realization of The Permanent Now and become Aware of your most accurate Self. The Permanent Now is where Watching Awareness, accurate Peace, Connection and **Y**ou live.

You are already Home.

Why do you chase and obsess with things? Things are temporary. Temporariness is a catalyst for suffering. Unveil Watching Awareness, which is the only permanent "thing" in this universe and Be your most accurate Self.

The Game of Hide and Seek is playing out in every second, of every minute, of every hour, of every day, of every week, of every month, of every year, of every decade for an entire human lifetime by over one hundred and eight billion individual human lifetimes with an ever-increasing level of suffering by the human species. The Game of Hide and Seek cannot be won from without. Read Insanity's definition, right now.

NOTE

Time-identification is believing TIME and the illusory reality/realm of past and future consciousness exist.

NOTE2

Stop self-identifying with and giving attachment to Time and all the illusions living in Time. By actively watching everything, leave the illusory reality/realm of past and future consciousness and literally Wake Up in The Permanent Now.

NOTE3

You let go by lowering your resistance to aspects of your inner self. You lower your resistance to aspects of your inner self by becoming more Aware. You become more Aware by paying attention and watching everything, especially everything on the inside. Then you can hug those internal issues. Lower resistance. Hug The Shadow.

DIRECT EXPERIENCE AND THINKING

NOTHING

Nothing is everywhere
Nothing is Something, just not a thing
Nothing is That which allows things to exist
Things arise within Nothing
You cannot grasp for Nothing
You cannot measure Nothing
You cannot know Nothing

Nothing is REAL LIFE
Nothing creates everything
Everything comes from Nothing
Everything goes back to Nothing
All things are a dream by Nothing
You are NOthing

NOTHING IS VERY MUCH SOMETHING

The mind is a tool. Part of the tool's usage is empirically measuring things like one meter, one second, one gram, this form and that form, etc. Spiritual Awakening is about unveiling Watching Awareness, which cannot be empirically measured and comprehended with thought consciousness. **This is the point**. Do not grasp for Awareness, your most accurate Self and NOthing through the filter of empiricism and thought consciousness. This will never happen, so why try. Listen for THE HERALDS OF NOW, step back from your mind and move through, past and out of self-identification with and attachment to Time and all the illusions living in Time and unveil Watching Awareness.

Awareness is beyond your mental foreground and has no end. ☺ ETERNITY AND INFINITY.

Just because NOthing cannot be empirically measured does not mean NOthing is non-existent. NOthing is THE SOURCE, the other half and the other side to SPACE, TIME and FORM. An aspect of NOthing is PURE POTENTIALITY and not the lack of anything. Come to the direct experience and realization for yourself that NOthing is all the above and so much more. ☺

You are already Home.

Conceptualization, Thinking and Relativeness

An inherent challenge in discussing the individual topics within the subject of Awakening, Reality and The Permanent Now is having you get through, past and out of mental conceptualization and thinking, which is Step Zero of four steps. Each step is an increase in the breadth and depth of your already consistent Awareness.

After reading The Permanent Now, a woman sternly asked, "Who taught you all this information!?" Smiling, I replied, "No one taught me this information. No one can be taught Reality and no one can teach Reality. Reality is simply Reality." ☺

Humans love teaching other humans thoughts, beliefs and ideas, which the first person wants the other person to believe in and therefore think their perception is Reality. Buddhas do not teach. Awakens provide accurate guidance to Seekers on how to come to their direct experience and realization of Awareness, The Permanent Now and their most accurate Self.

You do not learn Reality. You come to the direct experience and realization of Reality*. Ever since you were around twelve months old, you began learning representations pointing toward Reality. Because things are rarely ever directly in front of your face, you learn how to talk, read, communicate and therefore think in representations of Reality. You begin self-identifying with and attaching to the mind at around twelve months old.

You learn how to read, write, communicate and therefore think the representation of H_2O and you label the representation WATER. You constantly teach, learn and communicate these representations and therefore think and therefore live with and therefore live in these representations of Reality. Homo sapiens do proudly self-identify with the mind and thought consciousness.

The human species began talking, writing, reading, communicating, remembering and projecting these representations, which is thinking/mental activity, over two-hundred thousand years ago*[2]. The homo sapiens species has been living in the reality/realm of these representations for so long; humans believe this reality/realm is real. Humans use this reality/realm as definitive proof they are separate, different and some humans believe above all other life. The thing you call <insert your name here> lives in this illusory reality/realm. Every human lives in the reality/realm of Time, Thought, and the illusory past and future consciousness rather than being Watching Awareness and in The Permanent Now*[3].

An innate quality of every reality/realm is its own relativeness. The reality/realm of a deck of fifty-two playing cards has its own relativeness. Twos are twos because aces are aces. The reality/realm of games has its own relativeness. The one-eyed jack can change its relativeness in Poker. The reality/realm of counting repetitions while lifting weights has its own relativeness*4. Relativeness is fundamental to illusions, especially optical ones. ☺ Every reality/realm has its own relativeness because this is this and that is that. Even the reality/realm of this universe, and therefore everything in it has relativeness. Thanks, Mr. Maxwell and Mr. Einstein.

The reality/realm of self-identification with and attachment to thought consciousness has its own relativeness. If you think dogs are better than cats, the relativeness is small. One example, which is not small and is way, way, way down on the other side of the spectrum of relativeness of thought consciousness is religion.

This representation of reality, labeled religion, is not Reality. Thought/mental activity is not Reality. It is a mere representation. Humans teach and learn religion. You do not come to the direct experience and realization of religion. The Permanent Now is RELATIVE Reality. Your most accurate Self is ABSOLUTE Reality. The Permanent Now is where you come to the direct experience and realization of NOthing, Awareness and your most accurate Self, which is what the mental activity labeled religion is inaccurately representing.

When you touch, smell, see, hear and taste H_2O, you come to the direct experience and realization of what the signpost, WATER, is pointing.

H_2O is to the representation/mental activity labeled WATER as The Permanent Now and your most accurate Self is to the representation/mental activity labeled religion. The label WATER is not H_2O and the representation/mental activity labeled religion is not The Permanent Now and your most accurate Self.

The relativeness of the thought/mental activity labeled religion can be so strong people kill other life over its relativeness.

Upon leaving any specific reality/realm, the reality/realm no longer has absoluteness to it and the relativeness no longer matters. The one-eyed jack's relativeness is no longer important after you leave a poker game. A nightmare is no longer scary after you leave the reality/realm of the dream state.

After you leave the reality/realm of self-identification with and attachment to Time and thought consciousness, they no longer have absoluteness and relativeness to them. After you Wake Up, you come to the direct experience and realization thought/mental activity are all just things. **Y**ou are not of this universe. **Y**ou are Existence within and behind this universe. As for you scientifically oriented readers, ☺

"Science is a way of thinking much more than it is a body of knowledge". – Carl Sagan

Judgment is the catalyst for Relativeness within the reality/realm of thought consciousness. Watch for judgment. ☺

WETNESS AND AWAKENING

By talking or writing, teach someone and have him or her learn what wetness is. It cannot happen. When you immerse your hand, your toe or your entire body in water, does anyone have to teach you water has wetness?

No one can teach you one of the innate qualities of water is wetness. Through direct experience and realization, you get water has a quality labeled wetness*[5]. The difference is Awareness.

Awareness is direct experience and realization. You cannot teach or be taught Awareness, direct experience and realization. You are Aware of the wetness of water or you are not. Teaching and learning, which are always done through the process of Time and thought/mental activity, about an innate quality of water labeled wetness will never get you to the direct experience and realization of wetness.

As a noble, brave, sincere and attentive Seeker, this is the unveiling. Unveiling is the difference between self-identification with and attachment to Time and all the illusions living in Time and the direct experience and realization of The Permanent Now.

PUTTING UP WALLS, BARRIERS AND DIVISIONS

Around twelve months old on, humans put up illusory walls, barriers and divisions in their Awareness and begin constructing the thing they think they are. This is the beginnings of you resisting The Permanent Now and constraining, restricting and contracting your Awareness.

Humans live in an illusory world of comparing, contrasting and judging. Relativeness. Early human Awareness evolved from a radar-like scanning system used to detect differences, changes and anomalies in the environment and over a lot of integrative change or "time", this shallow breadth and depth of Awareness creates a myopic affinity and predisposition to X, illusory separating X from What Is and therefore, on an evolutionary-level time frame, allowing for the creation of the illusory individual me/ego.

After enough of these illusory walls, barriers and divisions are constructed, the illusory individual me/ego or <insert your name here> is built out, self-identified with, attached to and accepted as normal*[6]. The illusory individual me/ego, the illusory thinker thinking the thoughts and

<insert your name here> is everything inside your specific illusory walls, barriers and divisions. Everything outside your illusory walls, barriers and divisions is the rest of the universe.

Some fundamentally illusory walls, barriers and divisions humans construct, build-out, self-identify with, attach to and accept as normal are…

You construct the illusory body-identification wall, barrier and division. This creates the physical identity-wall, barrier and division of everything inside the physical body and everything outside the physical body.

You construct illusory mental walls, barriers and divisions existing of my thoughts. This creates the illusory self-identity-wall, barrier and division of me, my and mine.

You construct illusory time identity-walls, barriers and divisions, placing this most peculiar set of illusions on either side of The Permanent Now and step into and begin living in illusory past and future consciousness by self-identifying with and attaching to Time.

You construct the judgment identity-wall, barrier and division when you succumb to The Illusion of Separation, Uncomfortableness and Fear and place the illusory judgment identity-wall, barrier and division on your specific ideas, beliefs, value system, group, society, culture, etc.

To Awaken you must burn all these illusory walls, barriers and divisions down and step out of Time and self-identification with and attachment to thought consciousness and into direct experience and realization of The Permanent Now. Burn these illusions down by lowering resistance to aspects of your inner self and then hug this resistance. You do both by watching everything. Give more attention to attention.

NOTE

You do not learn Reality. You come to the direct experience and realization of Reality. Understandably so, humans appreciate Newton, Maxwell, Einstein and many others. They came to the direct experience and realization of parts of Reality, which they gave their attention. They showed, through the language of mathematics, an aspect of Reality so others could become Aware for themselves. As a language, mathematics has wonderful qualities allowing the language not to be affected by the change of human perspective.

NOTE2

Time and thought consciousness hypnotize all humans. Time-hypnotization and thought-hypnotization begin when you are around twelve months old.

This hypnotizing occurs when you give your personal authority away to the people and groups who raised you, i.e. your parents, the society you live in and the culture(s) you self-identify with and attach to.

Good news. You can unveil this time-hypnotization and thought-hypnotization by actively choosing to let it go by watching. Take back and regain your authority by watching. Watch everything, especially everything on the inside. Get out of time-identification and self-identification with and attachment to Thought and come to the direct experience and realization of The Permanent Now by watching everything.

NOTE3

Humans do not live in accurate Reality. Humans live in the separate and illusory reality/realm of past and future consciousness. The homo sapiens is the hominin credited with thought, mental cognition and conceptualization. Self-identification with and attachment to <insert your name here> is centered and rooted in the illusory reality/realm of past and future consciousness.

<u>Come to the direct experience and realization of this by being who you most accurately are using no mental activity; reading, talking, writing, projecting or remembering any representation of your most accurate Self right Here, right Now</u>.

We all know we are not the physical body. **Y**ou are the field of Watching Awareness, not the illusory thinker thinking the thoughts. Wake Up! Look in another's eyes and see **Y**ourself.

NOTE4

More on this in Chapter Twenty-one.

NOTE5

Two gaseous state atoms create a relationship with each other and wetness is a synergistic outcome. INTEGRATION! ☺!

NOTE6

It is like constructing a house into a home. A house is not a home until enough of the walls are erected, connected and tied together.

before you invent
your own personality
there's only I Am

doing will not get
you enlightenment, Watching
is the unveiling

THE HUMAN MIND

ENLIGHTENMENT

Then…

I tried and tried and couldn't think of a way to become enlightened

NOW…

After all and of course, It is your natural state

SELF-IDENTIFICATION WITH AND ATTACHMENT TO THE THINKER THINKING THE THOUGHTS

Human Awareness is extremely myopic. This myopia makes you perceive, believe and think in Time and believe you are the individual thinker thinking the thoughts. The individual thinker thinking the thoughts lives in Time. Your most accurate Self lives in The Permanent Now. When your myopic Awareness self-identifies with and attaches to Time and the individual thinker thinking the thoughts, you perceive you are a separate being in this universe. When used in any other way other than for reading, writing and arithmetic, etc., the human mind is resistance to The Permanent Now.

You begin resisting The Permanent Now around twelve months old. This resistance creates Time, the illusory individual thinker thinking the thoughts, the individual me/ego, Suffering, The Illusions of Separation and Duality and Fear, among other things. These illusions create more resistance, conflict and suffering. Crazy cyclical, huh? The Permanent Now becomes invisible when you self-identify with and attach to the illusory thinker thinking the thoughts.

REALITY

You cannot change who **Y**ou are. **Y**ou are Awareness. Human Awareness is very myopic and focuses on the foreground and what is right in front of your mental face.

MYOPIC HUMAN AWARENESS

Everything in the universe is a vibrational frequency*. You self-identify with and attach to the illusory entity thinking all the thoughts because the vibrational frequency you call <insert your name here> is tilted juuust a little bit and juuust enough askew from all the rest of the thoughts, mental activity or vibrational frequencies. Your myopic Awareness perceives the tilted and askew thought, mental activity or vibrational frequency to be the individual creating all the other thoughts[*2].

The tilted and askew mental vibrational frequency is just another style or type of vibrational frequency. Self-identification with and attachment to the illusory entity thinking the thoughts, the individual me/ego and <insert your name here>, etc. comes from myopic human Awareness. Your myopic Awareness perceives the unique style/type of vibrational frequency to be the creator of all the thoughts.

The illusory thinker thinking the thoughts is just a different type of vibrational frequency, Happening or experience.

This whole universe is an intricately woven tapestry of different styles and types of vibrational frequencies! ☺ Even the hard-vibrational frequencies, Matter, are highly repetitive and contained vibrational frequencies[*3].

It does not matter that one style/type of mental vibrational frequency or what humans call the thinker thinking all the thoughts, the individual me/ego and <insert your name here> is askew a little.

The thinker thinking the thoughts is just another type of vibrational frequency, Happening or experience. That is all it is.

Do you identify any specific wavelength of visible light as the creator of the entire spectrum of visible light more than any other wavelength of the same spectrum? This sounds highly inaccurate, correct? Because someone has an affinity toward the red wavelength of visible light, should this myopic affinity automatically make the red wavelength be the creator of all visible light and color?

Is it logical to assign the creation of all trees on this planet to the majestic Redwoods of northern California? This sounds highly inaccurate, correct? Because someone has an affinity toward this area of the spectrum of trees, labeled the Redwoods of northern California, should this myopic affinity automatically make these trees be the creator of all trees?

Can you see the self-centered myopia in this style of attachment? This myopic affinity and self-centeredness of human Awareness allows the human species to be unAware, immature and overly child-like in its behaviors, attitudes and perceptions*[4].

The illusory thinker thinking all the thoughts, the individual me/ego and <insert your name here> is just another type of vibrational frequency, happening or experience within your Awareness. That is all it is.

Human Inaccuracy, Misalignment and Fear

One example of inaccuracy, misalignment and therefore Fear within the human mind and human reality expresses itself <u>within the perspective</u> of The Second Law of Thermodynamics. "The Second Law of Thermodynamics is an expression of the tendency that over time, differences in temperature, pressure and chemical potential equalize in an isolated physical system. From the state of thermodynamic equilibrium, the law deduced the principle of the increase of **entropy**/(**chaos**) and explains the phenomenon of irreversibility in nature." – Wikipedia.

From the myopic human perspective, The Second Law of Thermodynamics shows entropy, chaos and disorder are obvious and evident in this universe.

Have you ever watched the following in a scientific documentary? While standing next to a newly painted iron gate, a newly painted wooden fence or sitting on the beach next to a recently built sandcastle, a scientist proclaims to his/her audience the new iron gate, the newly painted fence or the newly built sandcastle is order and the creation will move from order to entropy, chaos and disorder. There is an innate perspective of the human mind toward The Second Law of Thermodynamics.

This innateness tells you The Flow of the entire universe is entropic, chaotic and disorderly and <u>one thing</u> creates order amongst a universe of entropy, chaos and disorder. ?!Self-centered much!? Do you see The Illusion of Separation?

The human mind views its creations as orderly and The Flow of the universe as entropic, chaotic and disorderly. Therefore, The Flow of the universe moves the mind's creations of order to disorder. On the scale of this entire universe, are you Aware of the fear and self-centeredness within this perspective? This perspective is Resistance at a universal level.

Integration is at every breadth and depth within this universe. The contents of this universe are integrating in a positive and always forward evolution of The Permanent Now for almost fourteen billion years. Even the structure of this universe is constantly integrating. This universe would not still be around after almost fourteen billion years if entropy, chaos and disorder were accurate.

Only one thing in this universe is constantly resisting Reality and What Is. Are you accurately Aware of this thing for what it is? In addition, "…the law deduced the principle of the increase of entropy/(chaos) and explains the phenomenon of irreversibility in nature." is more accurately a broad-stroked, inverted, myopic, and negative perspective on Integration.

One example of myopic human Awareness on The Flow of the universe is through the perspective of The Second Law of Thermodynamics. This myopic perspective is inaccurate, inverted and negative because of the self-centeredness of the human mind and how it resists everything.

When you experience positive non-chaotic Happenings in your life, acknowledge and appreciate these Happenings.

There is an "irreversibility in nature." This universe does not un-integrate or un-arrange. The Strong, Weak and Electromagnetic Forces, Interactions or Relationships are the atomic integrators of this universe. The relationship of fusion and gravity, a star, is a Newtonian integrator of this universe*[5]. The Arrow of Time is Integration. You must change the breadth and depth of your internal Awareness.

MYOPIA

You self-identify with and attach to thoughts, feelings, values, beliefs and emotions, etc. because the human mind is the only thing you are Aware of within your mental Awareness. Human Awareness is extremely myopic. **Y**ou are "standing too close" to the individual me/ego. Therefore, your young, child-like and myopic Awareness self-identifies with and attaches to the illusion.

You are already Home.

One Millimeter in Front of Your Face Analogy

There is a person standing one millimeter in front of your face. The person tells you what to do, think and feel. Sometimes the person likes you and sometimes the person hates you. Because the person is so close, you have no other frames-of-reference and therefore you think the person is all there is. Step back from the person standing one millimeter in front of your face, the individual me/ego, and see you have been standing in a vast, empty and beautifully wide-open field of PURE AWARENESS-BLISS for your entire life.

"Gestalt psychology tries to understand the laws of our ability to acquire and maintain meaningful perceptions, *myopia, innate to self-identification with and attachment to the mind,* in an apparently chaotic world", *The Illusion of Separation.* My italics. – Wikipedia.

The Building You Think You Are Analogy

While smiling, you walk up the street and turn the corner. You bump into a woman standing face forward with her forehead, nose, chest and toes pressed into the tallest building around. You stop walking and hear her mumble, "I am this building. I am the material of this building. I am this building."

Compassionately listening to her beliefs, you are Aware she has been standing in front of this building for her entire life. You ask her if she would like to come to her direct experience and realization, she is not the building. She does not understand you. You tell her she is not the building she thinks she is. She asks you to prove this.

"I can't prove anything to you. You can prove it to yourself," you reply.
"How?" she asks with hesitancy and increasing uncomfortableness.
"Take a step back off the wall and look around," you reply.
"You must be crazy! I will cease to exist if I take a step back!" she responds.
"Do you see me here, with you, Now? I am not standing next to any building. Can you see I am OK?" you reply still smiling.
The woman does not respond. With her forehead, nose, chest and toes still firmly

> pressed up against the building, she turns her eyes back to the wall and begins mumbling, "I am this building. I am the material of this building. I am this building."

LINEARITY

The human mind exists within linearity or the reality/realm of linear nature. It believes in the structure of linearity or that Time exists. The mind teaches and learns through linearity; first grade, then second grade, then third grade, etc. The mind communicates through linearity: noun, verb and then predicate. It lives in linearity; the illusory reality/realm of past and future consciousness. It is trained on effort and reward, which has linear-ness.

A mouse in a maze. Learn the maze. Get the cheese.

Waking Up is not linear. Waking Up is so simple, the human mind does not believe or think it is possible. Using the word SIMPLE is not accurate. Simple suggests Waking Up is on a spectrum. The spectrum starts around easy and goes toward hard and simple is somewhere around easy. Waking Up is easier than easy. Easy suggests a doing. Waking Up is not a doing. Waking Up is non-linear and in The Permanent Now.

"Nothing worth having is easy to come by." – Unknown

Because nothing in the human mind's reality worth having is ever easy to obtain and everything comes through linearity, the human mind perceives a buddha as unknowledgeable or insane. If the objective the human mind wants is discovered to be easy, most humans will not want or value it.

If you choose to; Wake Up, spiritually Awaken, have no more suffering in your life, unveil your most accurate Self and live your most accurate life, you must increase the breadth and depth of your Awareness. Linearity makes the human mind become drone-like in its points-of-view of what it has come to expect based on what was and what will be. Do you see how the fundamental nature of the mind is constantly going from <u>then</u> to <u>then</u> and never in Now and therefore, does not understand accurate Stillness?

The reason the human mind thinks spiritual enlightenment, is obtainable later, after more work, preferably hard work, the harder the better!, is because this is how humans have modeled themselves. The mind's misperception on Awakening is trying to <u>do</u> some <u>thing</u> and connect with something in this universe. **Y**ou are not of this universe.

An analogy would be like trying to fly by strapping a bunch of feathers to your back and arms. It looks like it might work if the human mind could just somehow…at a later date…with more thought…and more work…and more and more. We know this to be an inaccurate way to fly or become flight.

What are you waiting for? Thinking will not Wake **Y**ou Up. Thinking will trap you in an unending and cyclical path within the human mind and self-identification with and attachment to Time and the illusory thinker thinking the thoughts.

When you come to the direct experience and realization of your myopic compulsion and fascination with Time and Thought, there will be a disconnection with the self-identification with and attachment to Time and all the illusions living in Time however brief it may be, at first. This disconnection grows longer, deeper, stronger and more still as your repetition of staying in accurate Reality increases. This can be the beginning of your awakening.

THE TOOL WHICH CREATES OTHER TOOLS

The mind is the tool, which creates all other tools. You can use The Tool two different ways. The only accurate way to use the mind is for reading, writing and arithmetic, etc.

An inaccurate way to use the mind is to self-identify with and attach to it and use it as thought to answer a question or solve a problem created by the human mind about a situation which is not happening Now. Are you Aware of this cyclical nature? Your mind is thought-form used to create more mental and physical form, which is used to find what Thought thinks peace is. Using suffering to get out of suffering. Crazy cyclical, huh?

The Mind as a Cage

Self-identification with and attachment to Time and all the illusions living in Time create the illusory mental cage of resistance. Nothing real is holding you in the cage. There is no cage! These illusions are seen for what they are when you watch everything and unveil The Permanent Now.

The bars of the illusory cage are the illusory past and future. The content of the bars, the iron, are the individual and personal thoughts each human chooses to self-identify with and attach to. The human mind needs and feeds on resistance. Self-identification with and attachment to the human mind is resistance. Resistance is necessary for self-identifying with and attaching to the human mind. The mind's structure falls away without resistance to The Permanent Now.

Judgment Creates Perception

Innate to the human mind is constant judgment and the reframing of stimulus into the perception the mind wants. The mind wants to satiate a past unresolved issue or self-identify with and attach to a future-based clinging.

"Perception is reality." – Unknown

Perception is not Reality. Reality is Reality. Perception bends, fades out and blocks Reality. Perception is the inaccurate focus of an unsettled mind and its very crude and myopic misrepresentation of Reality through the self-identification with and attachment to Time and all the illusions living in Time. When do you care more about perception than Reality? What cares more about perception than Reality?

EGO AND SOUL

Humans believe good thoughts come from the soul and bad thoughts come from the ego. Humans think the ego is the counterpart to the soul. More accurately, the ego is a label placed on a certain style or classification of thought, beliefs and actions. The soul is a label placed on the other style or classification of thought, beliefs and actions. Both styles and classifications of thought are used to represent the perceived origin of where humans think a certain thought comes.

No matter how you label your labels, the bottom line is all thought is mental activity. The ego versus soul perspective is another inaccuracy of the human mind represented in The Illusion of Duality. This inaccuracy perpetuates the lack of responsibility within humans.

The human mind is not bad or evil. It is a manifestation of your most accurate Self. It is a part of NOthing in motion.

The mind is operating in a system of resistance. It is severely trying to get Happiness and Connection in another and an other thing. **The human mind will never find lasting Happiness and Connection.** Would this drive you insane? It did with me. It drove me insane and then through, past and out of insanity and into The Permanent Now.

LABELS ARE INACCURATE

Is your hunger satisfied when you eat a picture of an apple? Can you quench your thirst with the word water? Can you climb the thought, tree? Can you accurately come to the direct experience and realization of the breadths and depths of What Is with any mere representation? No label or conceptualization can ever accurately describe What Is. Only being at rest and still in The Permanent Now can ever accurately help you come to the direct experience and realization of What Is.

The human mind tries to conquer anything it gives its attention. Conquering is mentally conceptualizing an object until a label can be placed in front of the object. The human mind's conceptualization and labeling of the object replaces all the living life the object radiates from within. The human mind has conquered the object and thinks it understands and knows all about the labeled object. It knows very little and is Aware of much less. A very superficial glossing over of thought by the human mind happens. Except for The Permanent Now and your most accurate Self, the human mind can wrap anything in thought and conceptualization.

Comparing and contrasting is innate to labeling. The thing is this because other things are that. Relativeness. Humans do not view Reality as It Is. Do not compare things and describe them relative to another. This is labeling. This is judgment. Watch how quick your mind does labeling and judgment.

Awakens are Aware of Reality which is not touched by labels and judgement. Awakens have internally developed, matured and grown up past the illusory reality/realm of labels and judgement and see What Is as It Is. Labeling, judgement and conceptualizing are part of what you need to be Aware of and go beyond. Go beyond these by being Aware when any labeling and judgment happens within.

REFERENCE POINTS

Because the reference points are too few, infrequent and not public enough, very few humans are Aware of the internal conflict being created when they resist The Permanent Now. When there is a reference point, a buddha, humans do one of several things.

First, the person looking for accurate Peace in his/her life becomes Aware of the reference point, The Light of

Awareness shining through the buddha, and the person increases the breadth and depth of their consistent internal self-Awareness. Second, the person who is deeply suffering gets very uncomfortable at the reference point because the reference point, The Light of Awareness shining through the buddha, does not give the human mind what it wants, which is a compatible vibrational frequency or resistance. Last, the other ninety-nine percent of humans are too busy trying to find Happiness and Connection in an illusory reality/realm to care.

The next time you are at a social gathering, watch the group. Watch the interpersonal dynamics of how everyone relates to each other, spoken and otherwise. When you do not get wrapped up in the social roles being played by people, watching the interpersonal dynamics of the group can be more fun than socializing.

DIS-EASE

Disease/dis·ease/(dĭ-zēz´) - any deviation from or interruption of the normal structure or function of any body part, organ or system which is manifested by a characteristic set of symptoms and signs and whose etiology, pathology and prognosis may be known or unknown. – Merriam Webster's Online Dictionary

What is the driving force behind dis-ease? What drives alcoholism? What drives obesity? What drives cancer?

What is the source behind these manifestations? What else are you Aware of which is any deviation from or interruption of the normal structure or function of any…system?

What are you Aware of which has a driving force behind it, which is never-ending and does not stop*[6]? What are you Aware of which is Imbalance? What are you Aware of which is resistance and mental suffering? Are resistance and mental suffering driving forces behind dis-ease?

You are ALL. The universe reflects on you, everything in you. The universe does not create from without and dump things on you. You might think this is truth. This is because you self-identify with and attach to thought consciousness and its innate outwardness.

ANTHROPOLOGICALLY SPEAKING

All life exhibits similar behavior. All life eats, lives somewhere and does something. What does the mind eat? It eats and lives on all the variations of resistance, conflict and suffering. Where does the human mind live? It lives in the illusory reality/realm of past and future consciousness. Most humans are not Aware of what it eats and where it lives, a breadth and depth of unconsciousness, because you swim in so much resistance, conflict and suffering all the time. What does the mind do? It constantly thinks, obsesses and talks about the past, the future, me, my, mine and resists The Permanent Now.

When the human mind's manifestations move from the mental realm into the physical realm, through the doings of the human body, the human mind is represented by the physical sufferings in the physical realm. What physical sufferings are you Aware of on a planetary, cultural, societal and personal level? What created those physical sufferings?

THE JUNGLE

Humans perceive this universe as separate, foreign and adversarial. This universe is not a separate thing, foreign or adversarial. This universe is your most accurate Self in motion. Which jungle do you think you left? While humans have climbed down from the physical trees and have left that realm of conflict, humans have not stepped out of the mental jungle of resistance, conflict and suffering. The mental jungle is the Illusion of Separation and the never-ending trial for survival and competition over a perceived another and an other.

You are already Home.

COMPETITION

Humans think, "If I can just be better than all the rest, then I'll be on top and be the best." From what point-of-view is this accurate? What creates this perspective? What will you win? What system are you the best at? You have become the best at doing resistance and conflict.

Because you are the best at resistance and conflict, what happens to you when you become the best at besting other entities in a system of conflict? What happens to everyone else, which you beat at the system of resistance and conflict?

Everyone suffers.

One side of the relationship thinks it suffers less because it is "better than" the other side of the relationship. Relativeness. <u>There is no other</u> and besting some perceived other in conflict creates more suffering for all, especially the winner. When things are given to the winner which the winner thinks will give him/her Happiness and Connection, the winner has a higher potentiality for staying in conflict.

Have you accurately observed what the "best" people's lives are like within this system the human mind has set up for itself and all other entities it encounters? These people are wealthy, famous and powerful, etc. These people have control over the resources of Space, Time and Form, which humans think they need for Happiness and Connection. <u>No human has accurate Peace and Connection</u>. Humans suffer inwardly and therefore feel a need to outwardly show the perception they are not suffering.

How much time will you give competition within the jungle? Are you waiting for something in the future to happen? ☺ You have all the time this universe gives anyone, right Now and this Moment. Get out of Competition by acknowledging Relativeness will not get you accurate Peace and Connection.

THE BUFFER ZONE

The human mind insulates itself from LIFE with a buffer zone. Some popular buffer zones are big bank accounts, big cars, big houses, big personalities, big relationships and big job titles, etc. All temporary things.

If the buffer zone is big enough, the human mind thinks it is safe from LIFE. LIFE is not a mindless machine or randomness you need to figure how to fit into or a test you need to pass to get into heaven. Awareness evolves into one last illusion to hide behind before the game of Hide and Seek is over.

THE CASTLE AND MOAT ANALOGY

> She builds a castle and moat because she is afraid of being attacked by some thing out there. The taller the walls and wider the moat, the safer she feels. Instead of walking freely with and as LIFE, she separates herself from ALL. She extracts herself from her perceived enemies and

accepts an illusory reality/realm of separation.

MIND CREATED SYSTEMS

Some systems the human mind creates are; capitalism, the education system and the social systems of work, entertainment, government, etc. These systems are based in and grow out of resistance to The Permanent Now.

The people who rise to the top of these systems are the best at competition and conflict. These people are the most unAware humans. Who else, other than the most unconscious humans, would spend their entire life beating up, through competition and conflict, another form of their most accurate Self?

These "leaders" keep the systems of conflict in place because of the rewards the systems give them. Some rewards are money, fame and power, etc. These rewards are all forms of outward leverage and control and things the mind thinks will give it Happiness and Connection. These systems are breeding grounds for humans to become more unconscious and more unAware of The Permanent Now.

Only The Permanent Now and unveiling your most accurate Self give you accurate Peace and unveil the, **already and of course,** existing Connection.

To succeed within any of the current systems above, you must win and conquer the other side of the relationship or you are unsuccessful. Are you Aware of this fundamental dynamic of the human species? Everyone can point fingers. Look within. Change only happens from within. Until you come to the direct experience and realization of this, not knowledgeable of this, there is no change.

GIVING UP RESPONSIBILITY

Humans give up personal responsibility quickly and easily. Humans give responsibility, power and personal control over to so many other things. Do not give your authority away. Come to your direct experience and realization of The Permanent Now and unveil Reality for yourself.

THE SCIENTIFIC METHOD

If you ever doubt the efficacies of Awakens' guidance and what Reality Is, is there a better method to use than the scientific method? Is it always Now? Yes. Can I find the past or future anywhere in this universe*7? No. I conclude the past and future are not in accurate Reality and therefore are illusory*8. My results align with my question. The Permanent Now. ☺!

If your response to the paragraph above is, "Yes, but…", this shows how hypnotized you are with the illusion of Time.

No one can observe the past or future anywhere in this universe. Everyone can observe integrative change in The Permanent Now everywhere in this universe, constantly.

Ecologist and biologist know when accurately describing an organism one must describe the organism-environment. There is only your most accurate Self.

Physics shows us quantum entanglement to be fact. This whole universe is One Thing, your most accurate Self in motion.

WHAT IS INTELLIGENCE?

"The true sign of intelligence is not knowledge but creativity." – Albert Einstein

Mr. Einstein's statement is not as accurate as it could be. A more accurate statement is, "The true sign of intelligence is not knowledge. It is the breadth and depth of your internal self-Awareness, allowing everything (including Creativity) to unveil itself." – FRITZ

IDOLATRY

From the Judeo-Christian and Islamic perspectives, self-identification with and attachment to Time and all the illusions living in Time is idolatry.

You are myopically worshiping TIME so much you think the illusion of TIME and all the illusions living in the illusion of TIME are real. Crazy cyclical, huh?

BY THE WAY

Consciousness does not come out of the human mind. Awareness is not derived by the human mind. You perceive this because you are not Awake. Because your Awareness is extremely myopic, you self-identify with and attach to Time and thought consciousness. Awareness is That which is the before-ness, during-ness, after-ness, beneath-ness, behind-ness and within-ness of all Space, Integrative Change and Form. Form, i.e., the human mind, does not create consciousness. Awareness manifests the relationship labeled Form and eventually the human mind.

The human mind identifies itself as/with consciousness. The human mind lives in/is Time. The human mind believes Time exists. Self-identification with and attachment to the human mind does create the illusion of past and future consciousness.

You understand Awareness is not located in the head or body, correct? Obviously, … correct???

NOTE

Everything in this universe is a vibrational frequency of the INFINITE and ETERNAL field of Watching Awareness,

STILLNESS and your most accurate Self. More on this in Chapter Fifteen.

NOTE2

William James', author of Principles of Psychology - 1890, "most puzzling puzzle" is solved. ☺! ☺!

NOTE3

Just like every other style/type or group/classification of vibrational frequencies, matter has its own spectrum. Matter's spectrum is the Periodic Table of Elements.

NOTE4

Connect this section to Chapter Fourteen's fourth paragraph.

NOTE5

All things have mutually arising parts to the relationship. More on this in Chapter Fifteen.

NOTE6

More on this in Chapter Sixteen.

NOTE7

This illusory thing labeled TIME, does not affect mathematics. Mathematics is about accurate Reality and what happens in The Permanent Now. Therefore, a highly inaccurate illusion does not affect Reality.

NOTE8

Intelligence and knowledge do not unveil Reality. Awareness unveils Reality.

the darkness you fear
are illusions of the mind
Watching drives out fear

astigmatism's
the blocking of light in eye
block is Thought as you

THOUGHT

Peace

Smile and look into another's eyes

Ninety-nine point nine plus percent of Thought is resistance to The Permanent Now, centered and rooted in Time and the illusory reality/realm of past and future consciousness and is about the illusory me, my and mine. Less than one-tenth of a percent of Thought is what Thought is. It is a tool used when needed for tool-related occurrences like reading, writing and arithmetic, etc.

Resistance to Balance

When Thought is self-identified with and attached to, resistance to The Permanent Now is created. This resistance permeates this universe. This resistance manifests in the behaviors humans choose and those behavioral outcomes. Settle out of the illusory reality/realm of past and future consciousness. Settle into balance, The Permanent Now. Be your most accurate Self. Be Watching Awareness.

ILLUSORY COMFORT

Self-identification with and attachment to Time and Thought is very comforting, compulsive and seductive. Illusory comfort is innate to Time and Thought. Where else can you filter Reality and make up your reality? Self-identification with and attachment to Time and Thought is like taking a painkiller right before you hit your face with a hammer. It kind of helps and not at all. ☺

Self-identification with and attachment to Thought and judgment create the comfort needed, which is emotion, feeling, belief, values, ideals, etc., for the mind to stay in illusory control. This illusory control is not accurate and covers manifested heaven, The Permanent Now.

Humans find a perceived and illusory-only comfort in conflict to be more rewarding than an actual guarantee of no more suffering. The human mind would rather sleep on a bed of known conflict rather than get up off the conflict and lay down in no more suffering.

I used to spend hours thinking and replaying thought-plays in my mind. I thought about how great my future would be. I hid in Thought, and thought was very comforting, compulsive and seductive. I faded out of The Permanent Now and wasted the only moment anyone has. I missed the mark of LIFE.

The assertions, beliefs and convictions "I am better than…" and "I am right about…" are extremely comforting, compulsive and seductive thoughts. Actively engage your Awareness in CLARITY and ACCURACY and leave Relativeness. This whole universe is One Thing, your most accurate Self in motion.

By Watching, accept Now over the choice of illusory mental comfort and begin releasing yourself from the illusory self-identification with and attachment to Time and all the illusions living in Time.

When you think about the illusory past or future, come to the direct experience and realization of the illusory comfortableness of what you are about to mentally self-identify with, attach to and make the active choice to stay Watching.

CONTROL

At some breadth and depth, you desire Control. You desire Control because you resist The Permanent Now and therefore, are afraid of this universe. You have a very innate and deep desire and drive to stay out of hell or fit into or control this perceived random, mindless and machine-like universe. Both perspectives are highly inaccurate dogmas.

You innately desire the control needed to lessen Suffering and obtain Happiness and Connection. This illusory control is over your illusory and perceived self, others and The Flow of LIFE. You are already in The Place you are looking for. Let go by watching everything and Be your most accurate Self.

CONTROLLING THOUGHT

Do not control the creation of Thought. Who and what wants to control anything except the human mind? Acknowledge and accept What Is passing through your Awareness and continue with Now. When a car passes you on the street, do you want to control it? Do you want to control the passing clouds in the sky? Do you want to control the birds flying through **Y**ou?

Why do you give emotional importance and energy to Thought? What thing is being emotional about the mind? Crazy cyclical, huh? Through direct experience and realization watch, observe and become Aware Form comes and goes. Thought, another type of form, has much less comfort, compulsion and seductiveness and no control over you when you are Watching, Observing and being the Awareness within and behind Thought.

ENERGY FOR THOUGHT

All thoughts are energy and therefore need constant energy input to be created, exist and stay around. Do not give energy to Thought. By watching and being Aware of Thought, watch your self-identification with and attachment to Thought lessen.

Eventually thoughts change. Thoughts are forms. All form is temporary. Form is created in Time and will uncreate in Time. Why invest so much in something so temporary? Watch humans who focus a lot on the illusory reality/realm of past and future consciousness. Do they radiate energy from within? Are you spending energy keeping the illusory past and future alive or are you spending a lot less energy living Here, Now?

Loosen the perceived grasp Thought has on **Y**ou by <u>turning into</u>, moving through, past and out of Thought. Do not resist Thought. Watch Thought and disconnect its comfort, compulsion, intensity, seductiveness, substantiality, and importance.

THOUGHT REALITY

Humans live in their own <u>there, then</u> reality. Awakens live in The Permanent Now and can hold different points-of-view while living in accurate Reality and not judging. **Y**ou are not a belief system, a set of values and roles to play. **Y**ou are PURE AWARENESS-BLISS. **Y**ou <u>carry</u> a set of ideals, values and a belief system within your Awareness. You play a role with this person and that person. You are not the beliefs, values and specific roles you play. You are PURE AWARENESS- BLISS.

Being in The Permanent Now is a state of Being, balance and natural-ness, which comes before self-identification with and attachment to Time and the illusory thinker thinking the thoughts. Being in The Permanent Now is the Being before you are being <insert your name here>. Being in The Permanent Now is not a set of laws, rules and beliefs. Thought is this.

Thought is a perspective. Thought is malleable. When thought is created, without Awareness within and behind the creation, Thought becomes real to humans. When Thought is created and there is Awareness within and behind the creation, self-identification with and attachment to Time and Thought does not happen.

CREATIVITY

The human mind can proudly think up any new thought-form. The human mind's thought-label for this is Creativity. This label is not accurate. What is represented with the thought-label Creativity is more accurately the resulting mental manifestation of the human mind's driving engine, The Want of Wanting More*. Applying the human mind's engine to the creation of thought will create a potentiality for thought consciousness, ad infinitum. Attaching creativity to the accepted illusion that the past and future exist creates a lot of potentialities and never-ending suffering occurs.

ACCURATE CREATIVITY

Accurate creativity starts with being Aware of Stillness in The Permanent Now. COME BACK TO NOW and have accurate creativity arise. There is very little partnering with Stillness on this planet. Very rarely, an accurately creative human comes along. Invariably, they talk about where their inspirations come. What do they say about the where of inspiration? ☺

CREATING IS EPHEMERAL

Form is created and therefore will have a moment of ending. Your most accurate Self is not created and therefore has no moment of beginning or ending. NO-thing-ness is not created.

Why would **You** want to self-identify with and give attachment to a thing? Things end! Have you always self-identified with and attached to every thought you think right now? Have your thoughts ever died to other perspectives?

What thing gets its self-identity from creating other forms? If you choose, you hold things in **You**. **You** are not those things

DOING AND CREATING

When you do, you create. This goes for both the physical and mental realm. There is a lot of doing on this planet. Doing is not good or bad. When the human mind does its doings, this planet suffers. When doing and creation are watched, harmony and balance reside. There is very little creation through Watching Awareness on this planet.

THINKING AND BEING

Humans are used to the amount of energy spent on thinking. People say, "It's hard to stop thinking." Do you see how insane this sounds? It is hard to stop doing??? Being is not dependent on Thought. Thought gets in the way of Being. Thoughts develop into beliefs, values, emotions, feelings, behaviors, etc. Thoughts develop into doings for humans. These doings will not get you to unveil accurate Peace and Connection.

Only unveiling your most accurate Self in The Permanent Now gets you accurate Peace and Connection. Do not think about what you learned in The Permanent Now. Be what you learned in The Permanent Now. Rocks, flowers and animals do not think about Being. They simply are. The human mind does not think about being resistance. It is resistance. Being your most accurate Self in The Permanent Now is much easier and takes much, much, much less energy than being a human.

DOING AND BEING

More doing will not get you to unveil Awareness, The Permanent Now, accurate Peace and Connection. Believing Waking Up is found through doing and linearity keeps you in a shallower state of Watching Awareness and attached to doing-identification and away from the reality of Being. When you choose to Be, you will probably need to be at rest. All your attention will be on your mental Awareness. After some simple repetition, you no longer need to be physically resting.

MEDITATION IS NOT BEING

When Awakening to your most accurate Self is your attention, any meditation other than Watching is highly inaccurate. Meditation is a doing and a tool helping unsettled human Awareness settle on one thing; one saying, one thought, one object and one behavior. If you want to awaken to your most accurate Self in The Permanent Now, you must drop all meditation other than Watching and fully let go of all and Be, Here, Now.

Do you want to let go of your ego trip that much?

MISUNDERSTANDING NO MORE THOUGHT

The biggest misunderstanding of no longer self-identifying with and attaching to Time and Thought is, "I won't be able to exist without my mind." This is inaccurate. When self-identification with and attachment to Time and Thought ceases to be the all within, Awareness shines outwardly and you align yourself with The Flow of this universe.

Mental stillness does not shut you down and have your interactions with Reality be mindless and robotic. Watching Awareness allows you to see this wonderful universe as It Is.

THE ILLUSORY YOU

Do not believe what the human mind and the voice in your head tells you. Do not get lost in the human mind's creations. Do not self-identify with and become attached to the illusory thinker thinking the thoughts. When you live in the illusory reality/realm of past or future consciousness and discuss if it is correct or incorrect, you have already missed out on LIFE. LIFE is The Permanent Now. It can be perceived the only accurate mistake you can make in this universe is to resist The Permanent Now and forget your most accurate Self.

Truth and Accuracy

The human mind created the concept of Truth to fend off inquiries, attacks and competition from other thoughts. This innateness of Thought helps secure self-identification with and attachment to Thought. This aspect and hue of Thought, Truth, passed through the gauntlet of judgment and Time and can be challenging to dis-identify with and let go. This innateness of Thought anchors you in the proverbial storms of what you think life is.

When Truth is self-identified with and attached to, along with the engine of the human mind and the human mind's label of creativity, infinite possibilities of options for my truth are created. Any wonder why there is so much human conflict? Focus less on the truth or falseness of something and shift your attention to the accuracy of a situation. Do not label things as true or false. Describe things with degrees of accuracy. Delete, dissolve and drop Fear by unveiling The Permanent Now.

The only thing real and accurate is That which is in The Permanent Now.

Linguistic Inaccuracy

Humans say, "This thought came across my mind." No, it did not! ☺ The thought went through your Watching Awareness. You would not be Aware of the thought and be able to say the sentence above if what was said was accurate. Thoughts go through **Y**ou. Thoughts go through Watching Awareness, not your mind.

Humans say, "You were on my mind all day, today." No, I was not! ☺ I was not on your mind. Find the mind and then show my Watching Awareness how to put the illusory me on your mind. The thought was "parked" in your Watching Awareness. The human mind is highly inaccurate unless it is used for tool-related happenings like reading, writing and arithmetic, etc. Do you see this? Are you Aware of this? Watch your language and voice and come to the direct experience and realization of all the other linguistic inaccuracies. ☺

THE ALMOST CLOSED SYSTEM OF THOUGHT

Have you ever felt like you cannot get out of your suffering no matter what you do? You cannot get out of any system by using the tools of the system to extricate yourself from the system. You cannot fly by pulling up your bootstraps. You might ask, "How can I get out of this!?" Great question! You must increase the breadth and depth of your Awareness.

If you are unAware you are under the control of something and that something gives you a choice between two things, you will not see the control because you think you are in control because of the ability to choose. The mind's two choices are the illusory past and future. You have another choice; Reality, The Permanent Now and Watching Awareness from within.

The Car Engine and The Butterfly Analogy

> A car engine is trying to become a butterfly by having the engine do a self-diagnostic test on itself. The engine will never transform into a butterfly and fly away. It will, with enough time, understand what the pings and rattles of the engine are and what the triggers are for the engine's suffering. The engine will never turn into a butterfly.

Thought in the Early Years

It takes mental activity to understand where natural resources are and where competition is for those natural resources. It takes mental activity to climb down from a tree, craft tools to safely harness those natural resources and create language to organize like-entities.

Over two-hundred thousand years later, mental activity has gone awry. Mental cognition is a tool used to help the constantly evolving human species evolve within the mental and physical realms. Mental activity has been overlooked, unchecked and unwatched for over two-hundred thousand years and is now controlling you and is what you think you are.

Mental cognition was vital for getting the human species' feet underneath itself, figuratively and literally, for controlling fire, creating the wheel and the other five simple machines, etc. The inability to control this doing has left the human species insane.

MENTAL WEIGHT AND RIGIDITY

Self-identification with and attachment to Thought creates mental weight. The thought, 2+2=4, has much less mental weight than, I am dying right here, right now. Mental weight and judgment keep you mentally rigid, in the illusory reality/realm of past and future consciousness and internally closed-off. More mental weight (the more you self-identify with and attach to Thought) along with more judgment keeps you very rigid. Religion anyone?

THOUGHT AND CONTEMPLATION

In The Permanent Now, you come to the direct experience and realization you can create mental form in harmony with The Permanent Now and not with what was or what might be. The outcomes of Thought and Contemplation are different. Thought is created based on what the illusory reality/realm of past or future consciousness is to the mind. Contemplation is created now for The Permanent Now.

UNCONSCIOUSNESS

Two major parts to Unconsciousness are; being unAware of the relationship you have with The Permanent Now and this entire universe and your self-identification with and attachment to Time and all the illusions living in Time.

In part, a reason the human species is so unconscious is humans do not pay attention to Nature, the universe and all the stuff outside the mind and the individual me/ego. Many humans are so unconscious and asleep in the illusory reality/realm of past and future consciousness, they are not even Here*2.

If you are sincere about Waking Up, no more daydreams and no more mentally wandering off. Stay Here, Now. You leave Now and depending on the deepness of the dream you can also leave Here.

If you are really into the illusory comforting dream of thought, you leave Here. This is when the potentiality for a physical accident quickly rises. In the illusory comforting dream of thought, you might stub your toe, cut your finger, wreck your car, run an oil tanker into Land or blow up an oil rig, nuclear power plants, cities or maybe the entire planet.

OPERATING SYSTEMS

Humans run on an operating system labeled thought consciousness. Awakens are Aware there is only Awareness.

A COMPUTER'S OPERATING SYSTEM ANALOGY

> A computer has many applications. The human mind is an application labeled Thought. This application has gone awry. The application thinks it is the operating system. It is not.
>
> Awakening is like rebooting your computer. Rebooting puts the overlooked, unchecked and unwatched application, Thought, back into realignment. The reboot erases nothing. The reboot creates space where the accurate operating system, Awareness, can Be without being masked by the overlooked, unchecked and unwatched application, Thought.

NOTE

More on this in Chapter Sixteen.

NOTE2

Depending on what scientific study you accept, the human mind creates a new thought, on average, every six seconds*[3]. For a human who is awake sixteen hours a day, that is an average of nine thousand six hundred thoughts per day. Are you Aware of nine thousand six hundred thoughts in your day?

If you are, fantastic. Prove this to yourself. On the back of the five cards you will create for yourself in Chapter Twenty-two, tally up each thought you are Aware of by putting a check mark on the back of the cards.

If you are not Aware of all nine thousand six hundred thoughts, can you understand the meaning behind one use of the word UNCONSCIOUS and how a buddha sees humans walking around in a dream state?

NOTE3

The mind creates so much because it is constantly using illusory past consciousness to filter Reality and cover up unresolved internal issues you have not dealt with and fully accepted*[4].

In addition, the mind uses the illusory future consciousness to resist Reality, try to control Reality and obtain all the future clingings you think, feel and believe will make your illusory identity whole and have you finally find Happiness and Connection.

NOTE4

You have become used to, numb to and unconscious to this repetitiousness, consistency and continuity of your internal mental chatter. This consistency helps your myopic, young and child-like Awareness blend the mental chatter into the background.

humans exist in
the relative world, this/that
all that is conflict

people tell stories
having conflict within them
Now has no conflict

CONFLICT

FREEDOM

Then…

An inalienable right of every life form

What I get after I have independent wealth

NOW…

An innateness of The Permanent Now

The origin of mental conflict is self-identification with and attachment to judgment and mental temporal movement out of The Permanent Now. Self-identifying with and attaching to Time and the illusory reality/realm of past and future consciousness is resistance to The Permanent Now. When you resist The Permanent Now, conflict arises and suffering is close behind. The origin of physical conflict is created through the origin of mental conflict. Until you Wake Up in The Permanent Now, your existence is based in Conflict and Suffering.

THE HUMAN CONDITION – another perspective

The following happens when humans resist The Permanent Now and myopically self-identify with and attach to Time and all the illusions living in Time.

One human self-identifies with and attaches to a thought. They believe in and hold on to this quite ephemeral and temporal thing. This myopic focus locks the illusory thought into place. Now, the human has entered the reality/realm of relativeness and the opportunity for Conflict rises sharply.

Another human self-identifies with and attaches to another thought, this quite ephemeral and temporal thing. The Illusion of Separation makes both humans perceive and believe the other mental form is from another and an other. Because of myopic human Awareness, everyone thinks "the other" should be leveraged against me, my and mine.

Now, there are two points-of-view and two perspectives. This creates dynamic conflict. Points-of-view and perspectives are ephemeral and temporal. Conflict creates perceived problems. Perceived problems create opportunities for solutions to be used to solve the illusory problem by creating more mental thought. These new thoughts create more positions, creating the opportunity for more leverage and resistance toward a perceived other.

On…and…on…and…on. Crazy cyclical, huh? This is the beginnings of being unAware or IGNORant to Reality.

If you were accurately Aware you could not find what you have been searching for, for over two-hundred thousand years, you would stop. Homo sapiens have searched (and it is not a search) for so many, many, many…many years. Do you see the cyclical nature of the mind and judgment? When are you Aware of this behavior in others and yourself? Do you know where you can look? ☺

Manifestations of Conflict

Vibrational frequencies attract similar vibrational frequencies. Like attracts like. When not used as the tool, which creates other tools the human mind is resistance to The Permanent Now and therefore lives in and is Conflict. The human mind thinks the things it searches for, finds and self-identifies with and attaches to are in line with what it wants. This is very accurate. The human mind looks at things causing conflict as things which can help ease its own conflict. This is one perspective of being unconscious.

"What you resist, persists." – Carl Jung

Three top killers for humans are poor diets, smoking cigarettes and drinking alcohol. These behaviors are outward manifestations of mental conflict, which is not accepting What Is or living "outside" The Permanent Now.

Most popularly, stress is relieved through these three behaviors. The human mind is in tune with these three behaviors because these behaviors create more resistance, conflict and suffering.

Stop eating processed food inside man-made containers and ingesting other types of poisons. Do not mentally hide behind food. **Be noble and brave.** Raw. Organic. Yum.

CULTURALLY

When humans leave the daily grind of conflict and competition within work and school, humans rest in entertainment. Humans create so many different entertainments. Stories humans create are:

1.) Man versus Man – conflict with a perceived other
2.) Man versus Nature – conflict with Reality or Nature
3.) Man versus Him/Herself – conflict within him/herself
4.) Drama – conflict with a perceived other(s)
5.) Action-Adventure – a story with external conflict

The human mind creates so many entertainments where conflict and successful competition over a perceived other is the goal.

Some humans forgo these types of conflict and competition and rest in other forms of entertainment. Some humans rest at bars and at home and drink alcohol and watch entertainment. Some minds are so bored with and used to normal levels of conflict they add more conflict into an already conflicting reality/realm. These humans bet money on the future-based outcome of the entertainment they are entertained by.

The United States' most popular professional sporting game is American football. Other than the game of war and the current system of business, is there another more conflict-based game out there being played by humans? When will humans see competitive events as wasteful? When will humans work together for the betterment of the entire species and planet and stop competing with another version of your most accurate Self?

These entertainments create more conflict and suffering for society. Are you Aware of this? When will humans develop mutually beneficial entertainments where the objectives and outcomes only have winners for all involved?

DID SOMEONE ORDER A BASKET OF IRONY?

Conflict-based games harness, sharpen and hone the competitiveness of the human mind. This perpetuates more conflict. Conflict is conflict. It does not matter if you dress it up, dress it down, capture it with a camera, put it on a television, movie screen or grass field. Everything the human mind touches is infused with conflict.

You are looking for a way out of your suffering. Do you see how much of the human world is based in conflict and suffering? Move through conflict by fully accepting ALL.

DRAMA

Drama is a culturally polished-up word for conflict. How much drama do you have in your life? Why is it there? Do you enjoy this conflict? Why? Do you want to let go of conflict and suffering forever or are you attracted to this energy? Other than the human mind, what else is out of balance within this universe? When you are inside the vibrational frequency known as Drama, why does this feeling make you feel relatively more important and relatively better than perceived others?

WAR

The human mind idolizes the stories, characters and relationship of the ultimate conflict. Peace through resistance, conflict and suffering, only in the human mind. Peace through resistance, conflict and suffering is a glorification of itself, by itself, for itself and about itself. ??Self-centered much?? ☺ Resistance, conflict and suffering are never accurate ways to relate to Reality or perceived adversaries. Do not fight the fighter.

non-acceptance of
Now is simple suffering
humans turn away

SUFFERING

SUFFERING

Then…

Everyone did it.

Most people complained about it.

NOW…

It is an illusion

It leaves with Waking Up and Awakening

It is not in The Permanent Now

Resisting The Permanent Now is suffering. You have been resisting The Permanent Now ever since you were around twelve months old. Non-acceptance of The Permanent Now is suffering. Self-identification with and attachment to Time and all the illusions living in Time is suffering.

Humans are used to so much suffering. You are unAware of how much suffering you carry around. Suffering to the human mind is like water to a fish. Because suffering is everywhere all the time and consistent with all the other people, as a species, humans do not grasp the breadth and depth of their situation.

PRESSURE

Do you feel fifteen pounds of physical pressure on your shoulders, right now? You do not because you are used to the air pressure on this planet. Humans are shouldering fifteen pounds of physical pressure on them, constantly, for an entire lifetime.

Humans mentally suffer and are so used to it, individually and collectively, as a species no one seems to be Aware. What would it be like to live without such constant pressure? Lightness of Being is wonderful.

HUMAN'S FALL FROM GRACE

The Judeo-Christian and Islamic story of Adam and Eve eating the fruit of knowledge is an allegory. Eating the fruit of knowledge did not push humankind out of The Garden of Eden. The story is allegorical. Humankind's fall from Grace, "leaving The Garden of Eden" and "eating the fruit of knowledge" comes at around twelve months old when every human begins learning and therefore starts self-identifying with and attaching to Time and all the illusions living in Time. The Garden of Eden is The Permanent Now.

Attention Parents

Keep your newborn child out of suffering and help the human species grow up and evolve past thought-identification and time-identification. Guide your newborn child to be Watching Awareness and do not hypnotize them with thought-identification and Time. Your child will grow up with no suffering and their Awareness will be extremely more accurate and more clear.

Technology

In part, technology is the ability to create a repeatable and desirable outcome using tools and the behaviors associated with those tools to obtain what the human mind thinks Happiness and Connection are.

At a higher level on the technological scale, the tools, behaviors and the corresponding results of those tools and behaviors become safer to the long-term existence of the user and more effective and efficient for the user using the technology. From the human mind's perspective, technology is used to create a better life. Awareness shows me, the previous sentence is code for, "What tool can I create to help me ease my suffering?"

Technology is useful for making people physically safe and getting humans out of mundane tasks. Movement up the technological scale will never get humans accurate Peace and Connection. Has technology accomplished this for humans? Will humans ever say, "Everything's fine! We're done creating better technology!"? The reason the human mind focuses on, uses and why so many humans put their hopes in technology is because the growth of technology parallels The Want of Wanting More.

DOCTOR'S NEEDLES

The more unconscious the human, the more the human self-identifies with and attaches to the illusory reality/realm of past and future consciousness, which is mental suffering. A simple example is, when a person is administered as shot, because of the perception of future-based physical pain, more physical pain is perceived in The Permanent Now because the human is mentally living in the perception before the pain occurs.

All the suffering and most of the pain is perceived about something, which is about to happen in the illusory reality/realm of future consciousness. Are you Aware of what is happening?

The mind brings illusory physical pain, also known as mental suffering, back from the illusory reality/realm of future consciousness and into The Permanent Now. This general process, in a myriad of situations, is what humans are constantly doing. Does this sound insane to you? It should. Watch yourself and see where else you do this in your daily life.

The pain of the needle prick is very insignificant. **Y**ou are not in pain. **Y**ou are not in the thought of pain. **Y**ou have pain in your Watching Awareness. Pain is within **Y**ou. Pain is one of the many, many, many things within your Watching Awareness. Come to the direct experience and realization of pain and put it in its proper position within **Y**ou.

Stepping back from Time and Thought cultivates Awareness. You come to the direct experience and realization of the fact **Y**ou are not Thought. This direct experience and realization helps put every thing into a more accurate perspective. When you are Aware of the illusion of thought and you consciously choose to not step into the mirage of whatever the human mind is masquerading around as, you can begin your awakening.

Awareness abides
Watching is the key to All
no past no future

there is only This
past and future are not real
there is only This

PAST AND FUTURE CONSCIOUSNESS

THE DREAM OF THOUGHT

Then…

It was seductive and normal

I lived in it

It was all there was

NOW…

It is the process and inventory of the human mind

It is born in time and not who I am

Self-identification with and attachment to; thought, mental cognition, the human mind, the individual me/ego, the thinker thinking the thoughts, <insert your name here> and mental suffering live in Time and the illusory reality/realm of past and future consciousness. Other than mental cognition for reading, writing and arithmetic, etc. go deeply into <u>every</u> thought you have and unveil <u>every</u> thought you self-identify with and attach to is centered and rooted in the illusory reality/realm of past and future consciousness. This alone can kick-start your awakening. You filter all of existence through past and future consciousness. You are literally sleeping in the illusory reality/realm of past and future consciousness. Homo sapiens believe these illusions are real because the entire species is hypnotizing themselves and each other with the spell of Time. There is only The Permanent Now.

You use all your past unresolved internal issues and all your future clingings as resistance to The Permanent Now. Unconsciously, you layer and apply this illusory consciousness on top of The Permanent Now and cover up The Permanent Now and your most accurate Self. Stop resisting The Permanent Now by filtering Reality with the illusory past and future consciousness. Let go of illusory control and have faith in your most accurate Self. Allow your most accurate Self to unveil your most accurate life.

It always has been, always is and always will be Now. Time and the illusory reality/realm of past and future consciousness are not real and are figments of your imagination given substantiality and importance by your young, child-like and myopic Awareness*. If you want to Awaken, you must grow up. There is only this Moment and It integrates from within Itself. After you come to this direct experience and realization, your awakening is beginning. **Be noble and brave.** Stay Here, Now.

Time is always Now. The past and future do not live on either side of The Present. There is nothing on the left and right of The Permanent Now. There is nothing on either side of this universe. When you come to this direct experience and realization, you will be on your hands and knees looking up at the sky happy-crying and laughing until you cannot breathe. The past and the future are illusory and only live in the imaginations of homo sapiens.

The story you call Time lives in The Permanent Now not on either side of The Permanent Now. The thing you call "the past" is the less integrated Now. The thing you call "the future" is the more integrated Now. **THIS IS NOT WORDSMITHING.**

The only real consciousness is Watching consciousness, Present Moment consciousness or Watching Awareness. On the other hand, Thought Consciousness, the thing humans are so evolutionarily proud of having compared to all other animals, is the illusory reality/realm of past and future consciousness and what thought is used for; reading, writing and arithmetic, etc.

Get out of the Time illusion and only use your mind for what it is, a tool that creates other tools. After you come to this direct experience and realization, your awakening is beginning. Past and future consciousness exists in the same reality/realm as The Easter Bunny, Santa Claus, The Tooth Fairy, unicorns, Satan, Gog and Magog, Shaitan, Pixiu, Grootslang, Yali, etc. All of these thought styles represent adherence to magical thinking, which is thinking, believing and acting upon a "truth" which cannot be observed.

When you choose to self-identify with and attach to the illusory reality/realm of past and future consciousness and let this illusory consciousness overlap, overcome and obscure Watching Awareness and The Permanent Now, you miss the mark of LIFE. You have faded out of Reality. You have been constantly doing this ever since you were around twelve months old. Actively let those illusions be where they are, in non-Reality, and let your most accurate Self Be in The Permanent Now.

Why do you take the illusory past and future and funnel them into The Permanent Now? The Permanent Now is not any of those thought projections. The future is not real and does not exist unless you self-identify with and attach to the illusory individual thinking the thoughts. The past is not real and does not exist unless you self-identify with and attach to the illusory individual thinking the thoughts.

The illusory thinker thinking the thoughts, the thing you think you are and your individual identity are thoughts within a place, which does not exist.

You are already Home.

PROBLEMS

Problems are imaginary. Problems only exist in the illusory reality/realm of past and future consciousness. They exist in the same reality/realm as The Easter Bunny, Santa Claus, The Tooth Fairy, unicorns, Satan, Gog and Magog, Shaitan, Pixiu, Grootslang, Yali, etc.

Change is constantly happening. When you resist Change and The Flow of the universe in The Permanent Now, you create illusory problems. Issues need addressing. Issues can only be accurately addressed when you live in Reality, The Permanent Now. Do not leverage the illusory future against The Permanent Now*[2].

Fully accept integrative change in The Permanent Now and watch this universe change from a place where you feel you must figure out how to get into heaven and stay out of hell or how you must figure out how to fit into this random, mindless and machine-like universe, which keeps chugging along with or without you and unveil The Permanent Now and manifested Heaven.

Past and Future – The Illusory Model

Humans perceive and believe Consciousness and Time are divided into the past, the Present and the future. The past and future do not exist. They are figments of your imagination. They are illusions. Only The Permanent Now exists. Only The Permanent Now consciousness exists, which is more accurately labeled Watching Awareness. Watching Awareness is your most accurate Self. Come to this direct experience and realization or not. Wake Up or not. Live your most accurate life or not. It is completely up to you.

The past and future are delusional thought projections. The past and future are temporal mental creations in The Permanent Now. Has anyone been to the past or future? Can you find the past or future in the universe!?

Watch a person walk across the room. Can you see a person's less integrated Now images trailing behind him/her right Now? Can you hear less integrated conversations when you enter a room right Now? Can you taste the meal you had last night when you enter your kitchen right Now? When you wake up in the morning, can you feel yesterday's sunset on your skin, Now? You cannot!! Why? Because only Now exists in accurate Reality.

How many humans grab hold of Time and the illusory reality/realm of past and future consciousness and grind it in their mind's teeth just for the sake of grinding? Nothing more. Just for the grinding. Just for the suffering. Grinding! Grinding! Grinding! And humans say they dislike suffering. What about you? Watch yourself moving into the illusory reality/realm of past and future consciousness and then COME BACK TO NOW.

GOOD AND BAD ENERGY

Energy from a friend is compatible energy and is wanted in the human mind's reality. Energy from a perceived enemy is not compatible energy and is not wanted in the human mind's reality. In The Permanent Now, energy is energy. There is no good or bad energy. In The Permanent Now, all energy is and is accepted. Acceptance is not agreeing with. Acceptance is not mentally turning away from and not resisting The Permanent Now.

Unveil through direct experience and realization, the reason you turn away from and resist The Permanent Now always resides in the illusory past or future consciousness. You must let go of your self-identification with and attachment to your past issues and future clingings.

CONDITIONALITY

The human mind is Conditionality. Accurate Love is innate to your most accurate Self. You do not have to do anything to have and give accurate Love. What part of you feels threatened by full acceptance? Go deeper into this. Unveil

Conditionality is an illusion based on a happening in the illusory reality/realm of past and future consciousness. Why are your behaviors centered in an illusion? Why are your behaviors not centered in The Permanent Now?

FUNDAMENTALLY DIFFERENT REALITIES

Awakens and humans live in fundamentally different realities. Humans live in an illusory and misaligned reality. Humans only live in the Here of Here and Now and many humans are starting to fade out of the Here. Awakens live in The Permanent Now. Go deeper into Now and your perspectives become a lot more impersonal and personal at the same time. Impersonal because you are Aware there is no real individual me and personal because you finally unveil your most accurate Self, PURE AWARENESS-BLISS – THE SOURCE constantly creat<u>ing</u> this universe.

BRINGING ILLUSIONS BACK

You go there, then and bring all those illusions back Here, and live them out, Now. <u>You bring illusory past and future internal issues back to The Permanent Now and live those illusory internal and temporal issues out</u>. You bring your issues and fears back into Reality and live them out. Humans are constantly doing this. Does this sound insane to you? This creates misalignment in The Permanent Now and because you self-identify with and attach to those inaccuracies of what you think LIFE is, you live this misalignment. <u>You missed the mark of LIFE</u>. The results of living this misalignment are resistance, conflict and suffering.

THE STREAM OF LIFE ANALOGY

With sheer exuberance, You dream and create an entire universe. Engagingly, **Y**ou jump in your raft and gently float down this universe's stream. Your dream ends when you get to the end of your stream. No one knows how long their stream is. This dynamic creates Engagement. Do not worry about staying dry or getting wet. This is a dream. Do not worry about anything. There is only this evolving Moment.

NOTE

Humanoids in all their iterations, from the ape to hominin transition, are five million years old and homo sapiens are around two-hundred thousand years old.

NOTE2

In the early twenty-first century, climate change needs addressing in The Permanent Now not in the illusory future. Climate change can only be effectively addressed when the situation is fully accepted. Do not turn away from the facts and hide in the illusory future. Do not leverage the illusory future against Reality and believe this way of thinking and this way of behavior produces desirable outcomes for this planet. It cannot. It will not. Leveraging the illusory future against The Permanent Now is insanity.

Humans love attacking an enormous array of things. Humans should unite and attack climate change. If unchecked, climate change will kill a lot more life on this planet than Mao Zedong, Josef Stalin and Adolf Hitler combined. After climate change, humans should stay united and attack the plastics plague.

separate from all
is the illusion you feel
quite inaccurate

THE ILLUSION OF SEPARATION

SEPARATION

Then…

What married people did after the kids grew up

A physical distance between two objects

NOW…

It is an illusion

It never happens

When you self-identify with and attach to Time and all the illusions living in Time, The Light of Awareness is blocked and The Illusion of Separation is accepted as reality and The Shadow is accepted and perceived as real.

Your most accurate Self is UNIFICATION and is not separate from anything. There is no accurate way you can be separate from your most accurate Self. How is this even possible? The Illusion of Separation is the most fundamental innateness of myopic human Awareness and self-identification with and attachment to Time and the human mind. The Illusion of Separation dissolves, disappears and is seen as an illusion when you consciously move back to The Permanent Now and Awaken.

The Illusion of Separation is the foundation upon which humans perceive and behave. The Illusion of Separation creates The Illusion of Duality. The evolution of The Illusion of Separation creates the illusory perception of the individual me/ego.

The human mind and myopic human Awareness live in an illusory world of comparing, contrasting and judging. Relativeness. This entire universe is Awareness in motion. Early human Awareness evolved from a radar-like scanning system used to detect differences, changes and anomalies in the environment and over a lot of integrative change or "time", this shallow breadth and depth of Awareness creates a myopic affinity and predisposition to X, illusory separating X from What Is and therefore, on an evolutionary-level time frame, allowing for the creation of the illusory individual me/ego. How can there accurately be this and that when in accurate Reality there is only This? The Illusion of Separation permeates into human's perception of Space, Time and Form.

You are not a separate individual. You are not a separate individual created by a separate god and trying to figure out a way to get into heaven or stay out of hell. You are not a separate individual created by the universe and trying to fit into this random, mindless and machine-like universe which keeps chugging along with or without you. These are highly inaccurate dogmas.

The Illusion of Separation creates the biggest illusion of all, the illusion of No More. Knowingly or unknowingly, the entire human species is motivated by the fear of No More or what humans call death. Read the middle part of Chapter Six, again.

THE STRUCTURE OF LANGUAGE HYPNOTIZES

The Illusion of Separation is shown in and perpetuated by the way humans structure language. The Subject-Verb-Object structure of Language hypnotizes humans into perceiving and therefore believing they and everything else in this universe are separate things doing separate actions to separate objects. This is highly inaccurate. Read the middle part of Chapter Six, again. In addition, the way humans structure Language is a telltale for the unconsciousness of humans and their complete lack of sincerity and attention for The Permanent Now.

Become more Aware of accurate Reality by watching Nature. Actively become more Aware of more innate nesses of Reality and eventually, if you **do not stop and do not expect**, your awakening is beginning.

The Permanent Now only has Happenings. Reality does not have separate things doing separate actions to separate objects! An inaccurate way to perceive, see and be Aware of Reality is through The Illusion of Separation and thusly separate things doing separate actions to separate objects. Nouns doing verbs to direct objects/predicates is extremely inaccurate.

One example of inaccuracy is, "The lightening flashed, and the thunder clapped." In accurate Reality, show me how this is possible. Show me the lightening doing the flashing. Show me the thunder doing the clapping. Show me the subject doing the verb. It is not possible. In accurate Reality, The Permanent Now, there is only flashing and clapping. A more accurate description is, "Flashing. Clapping."

Another example of inaccuracy is, "It's raining." Show me the subject of this sentence. It is not possible. In accurate Reality, The Permanent Now, there is only raining. A more accurate description is, "Raining." There are only Happenings! There is only RAINING.

Another example of inaccuracy is, "The rose bush grows roses." A more accurate description is, "ROSING." There are only Happenings! There is not a rose bush growing roses. There is only ROSING. The mind loves to dissect. There is no separation from your most accurate Self. How would this even be possible!? There is only **Y**ou.

Are you Aware that myopic human Awareness and the human mind and therefore language separates Reality into separate things doing separate actions to separate objects? Are you becoming more Aware of how humans innately and unconsciously live in the illusory reality/realm of past and future consciousness?

MISUNDERSTANDINGS ON INTEGRATIVE CHANGE AND EVOLUTION

The Illusion of Separation allows humans to perceive they are the static pinnacle of evolution. Homo sapiens are not the culmination of evolution. More accurately, what homo sapiens' myopic Awareness self-identifies with and attaches to, thought consciousness, is not the culmination of evolution. Unless you count your most accurate Self, there is no culmination or pinnacle to evolution or Integrative Change. Integrative Change is a constant, synergistic, one-way, positive and always forward evolution of The Permanent Now.

Integrative change and evolution happen in all four Kingdoms of scientific classification. The Mineral Kingdom has integrative change with carbon to diamond. When carbon integrates into diamond, the diamond does not change its fundamental material. While under enormous pressure and internal stress, carbon integrates a new relationship it has with itself to be an extremely different type of relationship relative to how simple carbon relates to itself and the synergistic outcome is a diamond.

The Plant Kingdom has integrative change by adding pollinators and flowers to plants. Pollinators and flowers integrate into plant relationships and the synergistic outcome are fruits, vegetables and honey. ☺! INTEGRATION is so wonderful.

The Animal Kingdom has caterpillars, beetles, frogs, etc. These species have integrative change from larvae, to pupa, to adult. Larvae, pupa and adults all have the same physical stuff and the stuff relates to itself quite differently. A caterpillar integrates a new relationship it has with itself to be an extremely different type of relationship and the synergistic outcome is a butterfly.

The Fungi Kingdom has mycelia, which are networks of underground filaments. These networks; exchange nourishment and communicate electro-chemically to ninety percent of all plants on Earth, have agency and synergistically interconnect, interweave and interdepend minerals, bacteria, plants and animals together. Fungi can affect events above ground and help integrative change and evolution happen in the Plant and Animal Kingdoms.

No Kingdom is separate from any other Kingdom. Separation is illusory.

There are around nine million cataloged species on Earth. Every one of these species is evolving in The Permanent Now*. One of these species is homo sapiens. Awakening is the next evolutionary step for homo sapiens. From Homo erectus to Homo sapiens to Homo Awareness. For over five thousand years, a new sprouting branch on The Tree of Evolution is growing.

HUMANS HAVE ALREADY MADE IT

The human mind thinks it has not made it and it <u>never</u> will think it has made it. Humans no longer live in the physical jungle. Humans are the apex species on this planet. There is nothing to fear outside or inside. ☺

Humans fear things humans think up. These fears exist in the illusory reality/realm of past and future consciousness. Mostly, humans fear other humans that do not think as they do. Relativeness. When will you stop resisting The Permanent Now and Wake Up to the Reality of What Is?

You can take the human out of the jungle. You cannot take "the jungle" out of the human mind unless the human unveils The Permanent Now. Then "the jungle" is shown for what it accurately is, The Illusion of Separation.

RELIGION

Fundamentally, religions state an individual <u>must believe</u> what the religion <u>teaches</u> or the individual is not a part of the group and the individual will not have salvation and peace in the <u>future</u>. Do you see religion as a style/type of thought consciousness? How connected and unified do you feel with this entire universe when you use Space, Time and Form to separate your illusory individual self from a perceived other? Religion inaccurately and illusory unifies a few and separates those few from ALL.

NOTE

Other than Reality, are you Aware of another place where Life evolves?

duality is

not in The Permanent Now

no duality

THE ILLUSION OF DUALITY

DUALITY

Then…

It was a tool of humor

It was an innateness of Existence

NOW…

It is in the reality/realm of the human mind

It is an illusion

The Illusion of Separation creates The Illusion of Duality. Myopic human Awareness perceives things are separate from one another. This is highly inaccurate. You perceive things as separate, opposing and dual because you resist The Permanent Now and therefore believe The Illusion of Separation is real. Humans perceive this universe as having a lot of separate things in it. Your most accurate Self is

UNIFICATION and has no duality. This universe is literally One Thing. This One Thing is your most accurate Self in motion.

"The word 'happiness' would lose its meaning if it were not balanced by sadness." – Carl Jung

THIS UNIVERSE IS RELATIONSHIP*

The Illusion of Duality is inaccurate because every thing in this universe is a mutually arising relationship and all relationships interconnect, interweave and interdepend*2. Broaden and deepen your Watching Awareness and unveil this mutually arising dynamic of all things. A thing is not one thing. A thing is a mutually arising relationship of two or more things relating to each other. This synergistic relationship creates the new thing. Watch Reality and unveil how everything in this universe interconnects, interweaves and interdepends on everything else in this universe. This universe is such a wondrously simple, intricate and dynamically complex integrative Play and Dance of intricately woven relationships of vibrational frequencies.

Below are this universe's most fundamental and foundational building blocks. Use these as a starting point and realize this universal dynamic for yourself and then continue seeing how this universal dynamic interconnects, interweaves and interdepends all things, ad infinitum, for the entire universe. Do not give your authority away. **Total fun!** ☺!

Before SPACE, TIME and FORM there is only your most accurate Self. With **sheer exuberance,** **Y**ou begin The Dream of integrative change. **BANG!** After a lot of cooling, energy slows down, FORM comes into existence, quarks coalesce and then protons and electrons, etc.

FORM

FORM is Structure and Content. Structure and Content's relationship is labeled FORM. This universe cannot have Structure without Content or Content without Structure. They are mutually arising. The following fundamental physical building blocks are a signpost and starting point showing how this universe is Relationship.

Less Accurate Observation	Accurate Observation
Up-quarks and down-quark*3	Relationship called proton
Proton and electron	Relationship called atom
Atom and atom	Relationship called molecule
Molecules and molecules	Relationship called cell
Electricity and magnetism	Relationship called light

A proton is the relationship quarks have with each other after they integrate and a synergistic outcome is an electron and the ability to relate to anything else in the universe. INTEGRATION. More accurately, three quarks are dynamically creating a relationship and the synergistic outcome is a relationship called protoning.

An atom is the relationship a proton and an electron have with each other after they integrate and a synergistic outcome is the ability to have a more complex relationship called a molecule. INTEGRATION. More accurately, a proton and an electron are dynamically creating a relationship and the synergistic outcome is a relationship called atoming.

A molecule is the relationship two or more atoms have with each other after they integrate and a synergistic outcome is the ability to have Newtonian-level structure and more dynamically complex relationships in this universe*[4]. INTEGRATION. More accurately, two or more atoms are dynamically creating a relationship and the synergistic outcome is a relationship called moleculing.

A cell is the relationship molecules have with each other after they integrate and a synergistic outcome is the ability to have a more complex relationship called LIFE. INTEGRATION. More accurately, molecules are dynamically creating a relationship and the synergistic outcome is a relationship called LIFE-ING.

These are inseparable aspects of mutually arising units, not opposites and separate. They must go together. This universe cannot have one without the other.

There are no naturally occurring only down-quarks in this universe. There must be up-quarks. There are no naturally occurring only protons in this universe. There must be electrons. These specific examples show you the most fundamental physical building blocks of this universe are not "blocks of matter." This universe is Relationship.

Light is the relationship electricity and magnetism have with each other after they integrate and a synergistic outcome are all the different wavelengths of Light in this universe from Radio to Gamma. INTEGRATION.

Every thing in this universe is Relationship. You cannot have Motion without STILLNESS. Examples go on ad infinitum. **Total fun!** ☺ Turtles all the way up and all the way down. By watching everything, unveil accurate relationships in The Permanent Now and watch what develops.

TIME

TIME is integrative change in The Permanent Now. When there is no change, "time" does not exist. There was no change or "time" before FORM existed and now there is change or "time" after FORM is dreamt into existence.

There was no change and now there is integrative change. FORM always comes from and goes back to NOthing. That amount of FORM's integrative change is TIME. You cannot have FORM without TIME and you cannot have TIME without FORM. They are mutually arising. TIME comes into existence when FORM comes into existence. FORM is manifested from the dream of NOthing and integrative change in The Permanent Now is mutually manifested.

SPACE

The here and there relationship is what humans label SPACE. Now that FORM and TIME are mutually manifesting, the mutually arising partners in the relationship labeled SPACE manifest into existence.

SPACE is That which a FORM in TIME is; above, below, right, left, in front of or behind another FORM. Nothingness is not SPACE. SPACE is the here-ness and the there-ness of two or more forms and the relativeness they have with each other*[5]. One form is above, below, right, left, in front of or behind the other form.

Up to now, this entire section describes SPACE, TIME and FORM without motion. Pretty bland, right!? When two or more forms and motion are Relationshiping, watch out! Boundless Synergies! **Total fun.** ☺!

This is the beginning of The Play and Dance of this universe! ☺ The playing and dancing of quarks and all the way up to what you label your life and beyond to the whole universe is your most accurate Self in motion. So wonderful!

In addition, the relationship of SPACE (here-ness and there-ness) and TIME (FORM and integrative change) is the relationship labeled SPACE-TIME, the most fundamental fabric of this universe. Furthermore, the relationship of FORM and SPACE-TIME is the relationship labeled Gravity. Examples go on ad infinitum. **Total fun!** ☺

Do you see how every relationship is interconnected, interwoven and interdependent with every other relationship? This most fundamental simplicity creates this universe's potentiality for complexity. If relationships were not so simple, Complexity could not keep becoming more complex. Therefore, total and complete INTEGRATION would not be fully accomplished throughout this universe's lifespan. Such a wondrously simple, intricate and dynamically complex integrative Play and Dance! ☺

LIGHT AND "dark"

A prominent concern for humans is how this universe interacts with you from the good versus bad perspective. There is no absolute evil or bad in this universe*[6]. There are only different hues of PURE AWARENESS-BLISS or LIGHT in this universe.

Another prominent concern for humans is how LIFE'S LIGHT and "dark" interconnect, interweave and interdepend with each other and interact with you. "dark" is not evil or bad. "dark" is a different hue of LIGHT.

LIFE'S game is Balance and Integration. Balance and Integration happen when LIGHT and "dark" interconnect, interweave and interdepend on each other. This universe could not constantly produce integrative, synergistic, one-way and positive change if LIGHT was always winning. A synergistic outcome of the relationship between LIGHT and "dark" is Change and Engagement. If LIGHT was always winning, Change and Engagement would not exist in this universe. Because humans suffer, humans want this paradigm. If "dark" was always winning, Change and Engagement would not exist in this universe. Change and Engagement are hidden jewels of this universe.

LIFE is about when LIGHT might win and "dark" might lose. LIFE is about when "dark" might win and LIGHT might lose. Balance and Integration happen when LIGHT and "dark" interconnect, interweave and interdepend on each other. This universe is not about LIGHT always winning. This universe is not about "dark" always winning. LIGHT and "dark" always interconnect, interweave and interdepend on each other and this relationship produces integrative, synergistic, one-way and positive change and engagement. LIGHT and "dark" are not separate and dual. Do you see this?

An eagle gains altitude and soars when it actively puts the forceful wind directly in front of itself. When "dark" enters your life, fully accept Change and actively engage living outside your comfort zones and come to the direct experience and realization of LIFE'S synergistic outcomes. Unveil the perceived "dark" winds of adversity are lifting you up, helping you gain altitude in your life and assisting you in soaring to new internal heights of Awareness.

After you unveil your most accurate Self, you unveil LIFE'S pure friendship. By watching everything, become more inclusive with your Watching Awareness and watch what develops.

Fully accept LIFE'S constant, integrative and positive change and embrace living outside your comfort zones.

HEAVEN AND HELL

After Waking Up, you come to the direct experience and realization there is no hell. Hell is a thought created by The Illusion of Duality and perpetuated by humans wanting to use the illusion as a control mechanism.

Get out of the illusory-only hell by unveiling The Permanent Now. The other half of the relationship to your most accurate Self is this universe, not hell. There is no hell.

Now, I am Aware I was in an illusory-only hell, which is resistance to The Permanent Now. I do not demonize the human mind. It is trying to do what you are doing when you read The Permanent Now. The human mind cannot get accurate Peace and Connection. It can never get accurate Peace and Connection. How can self-identifying with and attaching to an illusion ever get you accurate Peace and Connection? Other than using the mind as the tool which creates other tools, the human mind is resistance to accurate Peace and Connection.

CREATION AND EVOLUTION

The opposing perspectives of Creation versus Evolution are a practical example of The Illusion of Duality. Both sides look at the other side as false and present their side as true. Watch for truthfulness versus falseness in all situations. Instead of focusing on true versus false, which is based in the relative reality/realm of thought consciousness and Relativeness unveil the Clarity and Accuracy in the situation.

NOthing, PURE AWARENESS-BLISS and your most accurate Self did create this universe and **Y**ou started dreaming Motion and integrative change almost fourteen billion years ago. Motion comes from NOthing and through integration, we see all the myriad of evolutionary forms.

The opposing perspectives of Creation versus Evolution are somewhat accurate and not the entire landscape. The myopia of the human mind and how it views things as this or that, The Illusion of Duality, and not this and that, INTEGRATION, allows for these partial understandings and perspectives of the entire landscape. The Illusion of Duality sets my partial perspective against your partial perspective. Wake Up!

An inaccurate observation is creation versus evolution. A more accurate observation is the relationship labeled the entire landscape of creation and evolution.

THE TOTAL SPECTRUM

The colors of the rainbow are not only red, blue and green. The colors of the rainbow are not only indigo, violet, orange and yellow. The colors of the rainbow are all the colors. The comfortableness of my truth versus your falseness comes into existence when the mind feels separate and therefore afraid and therefore creates judgment and therefore enters the illusory reality/realm of relativeness and duality.

Come to the direct experience and realization when you dissect and polarize a relationship of Reality. The this versus that mentality is another example of Relativeness and Duality working within the reality/realm of the human mind, thought, mental cognition and conceptualization, etc.

The Illusory Model of Duality in Space, Time and Form

Leave The Almost Closed System of self-identification with and attachment to Time and all the illusions living in Time by becoming Aware of The Heralds of Now and come to the direct experience and realization…

1.) Space-based model of duality – Here versus there – What is right in front of your face is all there is.
2.) Time-based model of duality – Past and future – The Permanent Now is all there is.
3.) Form-based model of duality – Me versus another and an other – There are only different versions of your most accurate Self in motion.

In the illusory reality/realm of duality, things cannot just Be. They must oppose something else. Do you see the innate resistance to the human reality?

The Illusion of Duality in Personalities

Human personality is on a spectrum. The ends of the spectrum can be labeled the Bad Ass Me and the Poor Little Me. These examples show how humans use their personalities to navigate either of the two dogmas humans adhere to. As soon as you observe these from without, go from within and observe them within you. Seeking Control is an absolute misunderstanding of humans.

NOTE

This entire section is the real life practical application outcome to the Indra's Net metaphor.

NOTE2

Want to do something fun? Increase the breadth and depth of your Watching Awareness by creating a t-chart of all the mutually arising relationships in this universe. On the right and left side of the chart put the mutually arising "things" and in the middle put the "thing" the relationship is labeled. Increase the accuracy of your observations by cross-referencing your newly observed partnerships with the holonic hierarchy model. If the pairing is accurate, it will fit within its own holonic hierarchy. Coming to the direct experience and realization of the dynamics of how the t-chart is created and how this universe is woven together with Relationship is awesome. **Total fun!** ☺!

NOTE3

Ninety-nine percent of the weight of a proton is the force, interaction or relationship between two up-quarks and a down-quark. The last one percent is the quarks' weight*[7].

NOTE4

The Strong and Weak Forces, Interactions or Relationships are the relationships which build atomic-level structure in this universe and the Electromagnetic Force, Interaction or Relationship is the relationship which builds Newtonian-level structure in this universe.

NOTE5

Nothingness is dreaming SPACE, TIME and FORM.

NOTE6

The only thing relatively evil or bad in this universe is the resistance humans apply to; The Permanent Now, manifested PURE AWARENESS-BLISS, Change and The Flow of this universe*[8].

This universe is manifested heaven. When you resist The Permanent Now, you cover up PURE AWARENESS-BLISS and believe in an illusory-only hell or mindless randomness as the innateness of this universe. Then you spend your entire lifetime and as a species in over one hundred and eight billion different lifetimes trying to get out of something that does not accurately exist.

NOTE7

If humans build a sharper knife then CERN'S Large Hadron Collider, you will unveil the one percent, which is the weight of the quarks, is once again ninety-nine percent the force, interaction or relationship between the newly discovered particles making up each quark. Turtles all the way up and all the way down. It is amazing how much complexity comes from the simple and dynamic relationship of perceived dualities.

NOTE8

Ultimately, the thing labeled evil or bad by myopic human Awareness is the resistance humans apply to The Permanent Now. You can use this as a teaching tool and therefore is another hue of Light. ☺

want enlightenment
constantly get with what is
you're already Home

want of wanting more
engine of insanity
stop wanting more, Watch

THE WANT OF WANTING MORE

FUTURE

Then…

Where I kept my happiness and dreams
Where I spent half my life
Where everything will be better

NOW…

It is not real
It is illusory

The Want of Wanting More is the human mind's engine and driving force. The human mind does not want things. The human mind wants; wanting more. The human mind spends its entire life getting to the next thing. When the human mind gets the next thing, it is satisfied until it is not. The human mind wants the wanting of getting to the next thing. What do you suppose the human mind goes through on its deathbed? It looks forward to…? Yikes.

THE ENGINE AND DRIVING FORCE

Humans are always wanting more. Wanting more, wanting more and wanting more. Are humans accurately satisfied for any sustainable length of time with anything? Humans want; wanting more. Does this sound like dis-ease? As with everything in this universe, you get where you apply your attention.

To satisfy the mind's desire and want of wanting more, the human mind creates increasingly more complex, more detailed and more specific things which it thinks, hopes and believes will quench its insatiable desires. Watch for this within yourself. Observe the history of technology, especially the integrated circuit, and the general direction science and entertainment take.

The reason the human mind wants whatever is around the next corner is because it lives in the illusory reality/realm of past and future consciousness. Because of the duality-ness of thought, humans believe and hope the next thing will be better. The potential for the <u>flip</u> and the <u>flop</u> and the <u>this</u> and then the <u>that</u> makes The Want of Wanting More possible. Watch for this in your life. Observe how quickly you turn on a thing you felt you needed a while ago.

CAPITALISM

Capitalism works well with the human mind because fear and the need for growth is innate to Capitalism*. Capitalism cannot work without both. Are you Aware of the next integral and evolutionary social agreement after Capitalism? This social agreement will only work after a large minority of humans begin their awakening. Why? Competition, a dressed-up word for Fear, is a fundamental pillar of Capitalism. The next evolutionary step in social agreements is based on no necessity for growth and not fearing and competing with another version of your most accurate Self.

MONEY

Humans are so deeply self-identified with and attached to symbols humans think money is an actual resource. Money is not an actual resource. Money is an agreed-upon system for the tracking and accounting of the energy and effort humans give society and the corresponding rewards society gives back to that person for those behaviors and resulting outcomes. Humans say, "We don't have the money for homelessness, universal healthcare, global warming, etc."

The system of tracking and accounting labeled money is not a mature way of relating to each other. What is a mature way? Do not put the cart before the horse and move to the illusory future. Give attention to Waking Up and living in accurate Reality and let LIFE evolve.

The system of tracking and the accounting of human societal energies and efforts can be modified, updated or altogether changed. Change the system to balance and fairness. This change occurs after a large minority of humans begin their awakening. Eventually, if humans do not kill off themselves or the planet, the new system of tracking and accounting will be put into place and then will eventually end. Why will it end? The innate desire to account for and track "others" efforts will be seen as what it is. A lack of direct experience and realization of accurate Reality. Tracking and accounting systems are unnecessary when you have already come to the direct experience and realization there are only different versions of your most accurate Self.

If humans want to Be accurate Joy, Stillness and Love and unveil accurate Connection with the universe, humans must change the relationship they have with themselves. Humans must drop Time and begin trusting themselves, others and the universe. This happens with Awakening.

CONSUMPTION

Consuming more will not get you accurate Peace and Connection. Do not hide behind consumption.

HOARDING

The human mind thinks there is not enough. This perception creates mental and physical hoarding. Hoarding keeps you self-identifying with and attaching to materialism. Materialism keeps you self-identifying with and attaching to Form. Do other species keep their dead around?

NOT ENOUGH?

There is more than enough form in this universe for all. How many flowers are there for the pollinators? How many pollinators are there for the flowers? How much vegetation is there for the herbivores? How much light is there for the planet? How much solar energy can be harvested from the sun? How many stars in a galaxy? How many galaxies in the observable universe? Humans think…and…there is not enough. When do you think there is not enough? Where does the thought live? Come to the direct experience and realization of those perceived moments of lack and laugh out loud! ☺

WHAT IS NECESSARY?

The human mind says, "Necessity is the mother of invention." The mind's Want of Wanting More is another way of saying a constant need of needing. A constant need of needing is another way of labeling a driving force labeled Necessity. The human mind is constantly inventing new objects to find what it thinks will give it Happiness and Connection. Crazy cyclical, huh? Do you see the label the tool which creates other tools as more accurate? Technology is fine. Technology will not abate human suffering.

Mathematically Speaking

The mathematical equation representing the engine driving the human mind is exponential. Increasing levels of conflict and suffering arise within humans when the next step is taken by the human mind, from x=1 to x=2. What happens when x=200 moves to x=201? How many resources will be placed into the next step only to find accurate Connection and Peace are still not found? Is the graph of the world's population exponential? Is Moore's Law exponential? The human mind is never satisfied with What Is. The human mind is never satisfied with what it wants. The human mind exists within the continual journey and cyclical process of getting to the next thing. This search never ends.

Can you see how tiring and insane this is? The thought solution for the human mind's continual journey and cyclical process of never finding Happiness and Connection is continual peace forever or what humans call heaven. Manifested heaven is The Permanent Now. Unmanifested heaven is your most accurate Self.

Note

After accurately seeing the mind for what it is, the need for growth is accurately seen for what it is. The Want of Wanting More is an illusion within another illusion. Crazy cyclical, huh? The planet is a closed system. Competition is inaccurate. Subjugation of another for any reason including profit is inaccurate.

You are Awareness

You cannot change who you are

expand Awareness

the final outcome
is abiding Awareness
Laughter – Stillness – Love

AWARENESS

NOTHING

Then…

Everyone told me, "There's nothing worse than being nothing! You must be something!"

As time passed, I thought, "I can't be nothing. I have to be something!"

NOW…

I am absolutely Aware I am absolutely NOthing. ☺

PURE AWARENESS-BLISS is what is left when all things are gone. The breadths and depths of Awareness show me, I am Here and in The Permanent Now experiencing The Play and Dance of Space, Integrative Change and Form, while through direct experience and realization Aware I am none of them. The human mind is forever and constantly centered on itself. Awareness is not centered on any thing. Therefore, Awareness can be centered on ALL.

Awareness lives in the timeless Permanent Now. Self-identification with and attachment to; the individual me/ego, the thinker thinking the thoughts and <insert your name here>, etc. lives in Time and the illusory reality/realm of past and future consciousness.

THE LABELS CONSCIOUSNESS AND AWARENESS

For most people, the word CONSCIOUSNESS points toward the differentiation between animals and humans on a mental evolutionary scale. Humans have thought consciousness and some animals might not. Because of this labeling and social overlays, the word CONSCIOUSNESS is less accurate than the word AWARENESS. The Permanent Now uses the word AWARENESS and not the word CONSCIOUSNESS.

BREADTH AND DEPTH

As you unveil your Watching Awareness, you observe Awareness has two innate qualities labeled breadth and depth. The breadth of your Awareness increases your level of CLARITY toward your relationship with the universe. The depth of your Awareness increases your level of ACCURACY toward your relationship with the universe.

THE SOURCE CREATING THIS UNIVERSE

What is the energy source within and behind this universe? How do electrons keep their potentiality cloud, spin and charge for around a million-trillion-trillion (10^{36}) years?

How do up-quarks and a down-quark keep their charge and the relational energy needed to stick together and make a proton for around a million-trillion-trillion (10^{36}) years? From electrons, quarks and protons all the way up to you and beyond to the entire universe, how does this universe constantly keep integrating, expanding and growing for billions upon billions of years?

Everything in this universe is energy. $E=MC^2$ represents a certain level of Awareness, not knowledge, showing us everything in this universe is a different state or phase of energy*. Matter is a highly repetitive and focused energy, vibrational frequency and wave. Energy is not a highly repetitive and focused energy, vibrational frequency and wave. From electrons and protons all the way up to you and beyond to the constant integration, expansion and growth of this universe, what is THE SOURCE within and behind all this active and engaging energy?

Using an analogy, when you throw a rock into a pond, the energy wave created by the entering rock eventually dissipates because of the lack of constant energy being put into the pond. One rock equals one energy wave. A constant amount of rocks entering the pond equals constant energy waves in the pond. Do you see this!? Proverbial rocks are constantly being "thrown into" this proverbial pond-universe creating, expanding and growing this universe*2.

With **sheer exuberance**, your most accurate Self is THE SOURCE constantly manifesting, energizing and creating this entire universe. Your most accurate Self is never separate from anything.

TIME IS AN ILLUSION

Time does not roll, flow or move from the future into Reality and then roll, flow or move from Reality into the past or vice versa. You think Time is linear because you live in the illusory linear reality/realm of past and future consciousness.

Now is all there is. There is nothing outside or on either side of The Permanent Now. After you Awaken, you come to this direct experience and realization. It is awesome. Highly liberating. ☺ I happy-cried a lot.

This non-linear structure of the universe allows your most accurate Self, PURE AWARENESS-BLISS, to have an almost limitless potential for the evolution and integration of The Permanent Now.

The universe's structure allows your most accurate Self, PURE AWARENESS-BLISS, to manifest whatever needs to be for you to have The Dream you call your life and this universe. This structure is the only way there can be no problems in The Permanent Now.

If Time was real, the lack of potentiality would be catastrophically claustrophobic!

This direct experience and realization of the accurate structure and flow of integrative change/"time" and how this universe integrates from within Itself allows you to accurately live in The Permanent Now without fear. It always was Now. It always is Now. It always will be Now and THERE ARE NO PROBLEMS NOW. ☺! ☺!

REALITY

The Permanent Now is invisible to humans. Humans describe time reality in this manner…

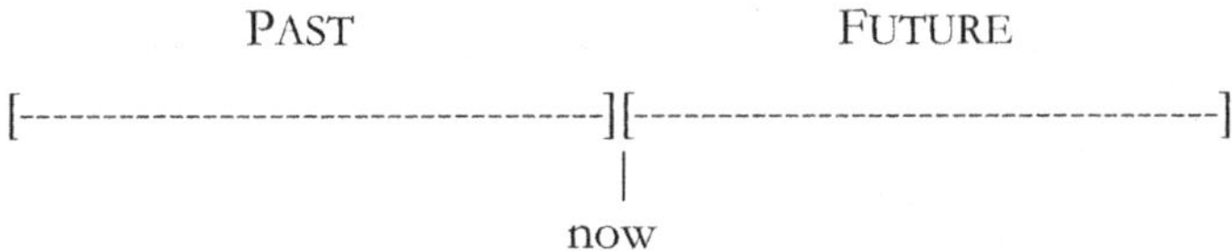

After you Awaken, you come to the direct experience and realization that Reality is…

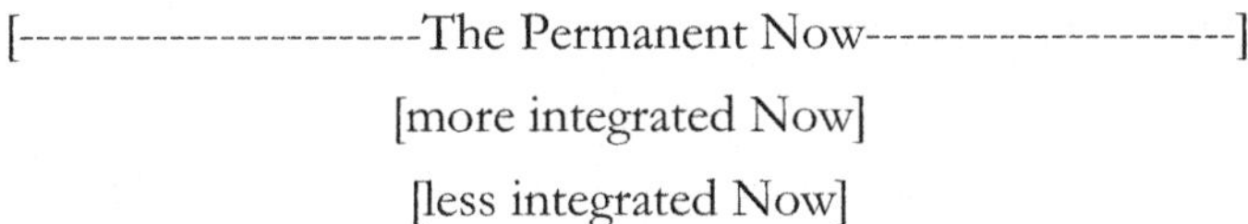

The illusory reality/realm of past and future consciousness only exists when you choose to self-identify with and attach to the individual me/ego, the thinker thinking the thoughts and <insert your name here>, etc. The story you create labeled Time is quite ephemeral and always in The Permanent Now. You cannot leave, escape or run from The Permanent Now. THERE ARE NO PROBLEMS NOW. Why do you resist and "leave" manifested heaven?

Instead of perceiving Time as linear, come to the direct experience and realization Time is the integration of motion and Form within Space always in The Permanent Now. This integrative change is what you perceive as Time. You mentally create the linear reality/realm of Time when you resist The Permanent Now and therefore self-identify with and become attached to Time and all the illusions living in Time. This self-identification and attachment myopically bends your Awareness and you perceive integrative change as the illusory past and future.

THE UNIVERSE WORKS IN MYSTERIOUS WAYS

The reason the saying, "The universe works in mysterious ways," has the word MYSTERIOUS in it is humans only know about linear-ness or the reality/realm of linearity. More accurately, "Your most accurate Self works in a non-linear fashion." Literally Wake Up in The Permanent Now and find out for yourself. Be your most accurate Self. Be Watching Awareness. Do this by watching everything.

SPIRIT, PURE AWARENESS-BLISS, ETC.

Spirit is another label for your most accurate Self. Spirit is not a concept and cannot be understood through thought.

If your thought style is Agnostic, you can see Spirit as a Higher Power. If your thought style is Atheist, you can see Spirit as ALL, NOthing and PURE AWARENESS-BLISS. If your thought style is Buddhist, you can see Spirit as Nirvana, Zen and The Tao. If your thought style is Christian, you can see Spirit as god and heaven in union. If your thought style is Hindu, you can see Spirit as Brahman, Atman and Supreme Identity. If your thought style is Islamic, you can see Spirit as Jannah/Firdaus. If your thought style is Scientific, you can see Spirit as zero net total energy of the universe. And for everyone; The Self, THE SOURCE creat<u>ing</u> this universe, Ultimate Union, Being, NOthing, The Unquantifiable, The Unknowable and Absolute Stillness. Spirit, PURE AWARENESS-BLISS and your most accurate Self have no voice and cannot speak.

COMPASSION

ALL IS FORGIVEN

Accurate and <u>lasting</u> compassion is the direct experience and realization of where ALL comes. That other person over there, that other life form over there and that other thing over there is a different version of your most accurate Self. The next time you raise your voice or your hand to another realize you are raising your voice or your hand to yourself. Literally.

When you raise your voice or hand mentally or physically to another version of your most accurate Self, unless the person is an Awaken, you create more Shadow for the other version of your most accurate Self. Crazy cyclical, huh?

Humans are unAware in and completely unAware of The Permanent Now. Humans think Time is real. Humans act in Time. Humans think they were born and will die. Humans think they are the quite ephemeral body and mind. Humans are hypnotized by and therefore believe in and therefore are controlled by an illusion living in an illusory reality/realm. Crazy cyclical, huh?

Humans older than around twelve months have no direct experience and realization of their most accurate Self. Humans have no direct experience and realization this entire universe is a dream of **sheer exuberance** by their most accurate Self. Humans have no direct experience and realization of what REAL JOY, STILLNESS, LOVE, CLARITY, ACCURACY and PERMANENCE are. Humans have no direct experience and realization of what **REAL LIFE** is. Etc. How can a buddha not have compassion for the only insane species on the planet?

I am Aware of what you are going through. I was once there, as well. All the best.

THE FLOW

Very rarely, a physical or mental athlete talks about peaking during a highly competitive event. They call this peaking attaining The Flow*3. The Flow is the normal structure of this universe. Wake Up and come to the direct experience and realization you are already in The Flow if you stop resisting The Permanent Now.

Stop resisting The Permanent Now by lowering resistance to aspects of your inner self you do not want to fully accept and deal with. You come to the direct experience and realization of this internal resistance and then lower this internal resistance by watching everything. After this internal resistance is lowered, fully accept those aspects of your inner self and come to the direct experience and realization that The Flow is already here. You do not attain The Flow. Let go of your resistance to The Permanent Now and come to the direct experience and realization The Flow is **already and of course** always happening.

TOTAL REALITY IS LIKE A WATER FOUNTAIN

A water fountain has a reservoir of water in which the fountain's water movements are drawn. The reservoir where the water movements come from is the realm of Stillness and No Motion. Absolute Reality and your most accurate Self is the realm of Stillness and No Motion.

The water movements, which are constantly being created from the fountain's reservoir, become the individual movements of the water fountain. Above the fountain's reservoir is Motion. A wonderous water fountain. This universe is the realm of relative reality and Motion.

Humans are not Aware of the Absolute Realm because humans live in the illusory reality/realm of past and future consciousness. Humans do not even know this relative Reality, The Permanent Now. If you did, you would have come to the direct experience and realization of your most accurate Self within this relative Reality and have already shed Time, Fear and Suffering and laughed out loud about how much complexity comes from NOTHING!! ☺!

From Stillness comes Motion comes LIFE into this reality/realm of Space, Integrative Change and Form. This universe. Motion stays for a while and then falls back into Stillness to be reborn again and again and again as Motion. Easily see this at this universe's quantum level. This happens at the Newtonian level, as well. It is a bit more challenging to see because integrative change at the Newtonian level is slower and less frequent than at the quantum level.

There is only **You**. Find a water fountain, sit down in front of it and watch.

PIGGYBACKING – THE GREAT USURPER

The piggybacking behavior of the human mind towards the constant integration of The Permanent Now is the most amazing camouflage of any entity on this entire planet. When a Happening occurs in life, the human mind positions itself into an ownership role of the Happening by bending the perspective of the situation into a situation where your myopic human Awareness thinks and believes the mind is responsible for the Happening*4. This is a large part of how you perceive and believe the illusory thinker thinking the thoughts is real.

The mind did not do the happening. The illusory thinker thinking the thoughts is not real. It is an illusion that is juuust a bit askew from all the rest of the thoughts to make your myopic Awareness believe it is who you are. Unveil Watching Awareness and come to this direct experience and realization yourself. The individual me/ego does not have control because the individual me/ego does not exist.

Write out on a piece of paper, how your mind, internally, not physically, makes a fist, grows your hair and blinks, etc.

PERSONAL ACCOUNTABILITY

You must be Aware and understand you are the only one responsible for your awakening. Another place, time, individual, thought or thing cannot help you. Only **You**. Only Here. Only Now.

Pizza Anyone Analogy

I worked for a company where over ninety-eight percent of the people worked in vast fields of cubicles on vast open floors. Almost everyone worked through lunch. I routinely saw one specific employee have pizza delivered to his desk for lunch. I also routinely saw other people around this gentleman look upon his actions with astonishment, bewilderment and surprise.

I heard them whisper behind his back, "Who does he think he is? How can he get to do that? I can't do that! His pizza looks so nice and all I have is this lousy sandwich." Occasionally, I watched someone bravely walk up to his cubicle and ask him, "How did you get that pizza?" Every single time he was asked, he replied smiling, "I called the pizza place. They deliver here. I even checked with our manager's manager. She said it was fine. Anyone can do this. It is not hard. All you have to do is make the call."

People did not believe him. Rarely, some people asked him if he would make the call for them. He replied, "I'm not going to make your call for you. You can do that yourself." Nobody did.

One day, a colleague of his took him up on his advice. That day two people had pizza at their desks. Both people were quite happy with what transpired. Everyone else was still astonished, bewildered and surprised! Some were even mad at the two of them for having something they thought they could never have.

I heard one woman get mad at the other employee and say, "How dare she get a pizza like him. She's not special like he is. She's such a bitch!" It was an interesting scene to watch.

If you think you cannot have or are not inalienably entitled to a life of no more suffering, you will not. You are wonderful and worthy.

MISUNDERSTANDING AWAKENS

Humans commonly misunderstand an Awaken as always happy. This is not entirely accurate. This misunderstanding comes from The Illusion of Duality. The human mind thinks if someone is not suffering, they must be happy. The reality an Awaken lives in is ALL. Joy, Stillness and Love are the only real emotions because all are breadths, depths and hues of Awareness.

The perception of an Awaken not wanting is not entirely accurate. It is not that an Awaken does not want. The Want of Wanting More has shown itself to be what it accurately is, an illusion within an illusion. Crazy cyclical, huh? Awakens are peacefully satisfied with What Is.

Before I Woke Up, I thought a buddha's attitude was, wanting to accept less. Can you see the structure of the last sentence is the exact structure of the human mind? The only thing which has changed was the content. Come to the direct experience and realization of the tricks the human mind uses and be well on your way to unveiling your most accurate Self. Awakens accept What Is. Move toward conscious, active and internal nurturing of Watching Awareness within and behind everything.

Humans usually think a buddha is settling for less. An Awaken is accurately Aware (s)he is accepting What Is. Only after full acceptance of What Is, can accurate, effective, conscious, active and internal nurturing of Watching Awareness from within, for one's internal state within and behind every behavior an individual takes, help create what might come. Are you doing the above repeatedly in the Present? ☺

PAY ATTENTION

People say how wonderful their life seems to go when they pay attention. Paying attention is natural. Everything on this planet pays attention except humans. Natural is manifested heaven. Not paying attention is not natural. Not natural is another way of saying, your mind takes over, it resists natural and you suffer. Pay attention! ☺ Apply attention to What Is not to what is not.

GROCERY STORE SHELVES

Everyone is Aware of an object placed right in front of his/her face, unless the human is so myopically focused on thought, they are not Here of the Here and Now. When you are at the grocery store and you are looking for an item on the shelf, you look and look and you cannot find the item and then voila you see the item. It was always there; you did not see the item until you returned to the Here of Here and Now. You do not see the item because you are lost in the illusory reality/realm of past and future consciousness.

When a human is there, then, miscommunications and mental and physical accidents happen. The human species is getting so deep into the illusory reality/realm of past and future consciousness the amount of accidents, per unit of measure is increasing exponentially.

THINGS GO THROUGH YOU

You are Awareness. Things go through your Awareness. Things go through **Y**ou. You see things go through **Y**ou. Clouds go through **Y**ou. You hear things go through **Y**ou. Sounds of a chirping bird go through **Y**ou. There is no sound. There is a sound. There is no sound.

Matter, highly focused and repetitive energy, "parks in" **Y**ou and stays awhile. Normal energy moves right through **Y**ou without stopping. You are Aware of these things. You are Aware you are not these things simply, exactly and precisely because you are Aware of them.

Feelings and emotions are within your body and Awareness. These feelings and emotions, the vibrational connections between the mind and the body come, "park in" **Y**ou for a while and then go. Just like everything, feelings and emotions always come and go. **Y**ou are the Awareness behind those feelings and emotions. Simply, exactly and precisely because you are Aware of those feelings and emotions, you cannot Be those feelings and emotions or you could not distinguish between **Y**ou and the feelings and emotions.

Thoughts move through your Awareness. **Y**ou are the Awareness behind your thoughts. Just like everything, thoughts come, "park in" **Y**ou for a while and then go. Thoughts always come and then leave. You are Aware of these thoughts. Simply, exactly and precisely because you are the Awareness behind these thoughts, you cannot be these thoughts or you would not be able to distinguish between **Y**ou and the thoughts coming and going.

Do not just use your sense of smell, taste, touch, hearing and sight. Be the Awareness within and behind the senses. Do not just see a thing. Be the Awareness behind Sight. **Total fun!** Apply attention, sincerity and repetition to watching everything and let go of what you think you are and accurately come to the direct experience and realization of your most accurate Self.

AWARENESS AND UNCONSCIOUSNESS

Because everyone is creating so many things, humans are unAware of and therefore do not acknowledge all the things they create. When you are in a place where everyone is doing so many doings like everyone else, everything and everyone seems normal. How can you slow down? Watch everything.

DO YOU SEE THIS?

Do you see how every one of these different labels, identities and attachments; thought, the human mind, the individual me/ego, the thinker thinking the thoughts, the illusory reality/realm of past and future consciousness, <insert your name here> and mental suffering exist in the same illusion labeled Time? Come to the direct experience and realization all these labels, identities and attachments are in the illusion of Time and begin your awakening.

MOVIE ANALOGY

Your most accurate Self is
the projector and the director
the cast and the crew
there is only **You**
the screen and the scene
do you see what I mean

THERE IS ONLY HAPPENING, EXPERIENCING AND THIS-ING

Every quark to every atom to every molecule to every amino acid to every peptide and protein to every cell to every plant to every animal, ad infinitum throughout the universe, etc. is Watching Awareness at that specific level of existence. **There is only PURE-AWARENESS** in this universe. This entire universe is made up of different Happenings, Experiencings and This-ings of PURE AWARENESS.

This entire universe, your most accurate Self in motion, is having Happenings, Experiencings and This-ings at that specific level/area of existing.

Rocks are Awareness in motion and Awareness-ING at the level of rocks. A more accurate description is, "ROCK-ING." If you hit a rock, it will relate to you albeit at a level less than an animal.

Plants and animals are Awareness in motion and Awareness-ING. A more accurate description is, "PLANT-ING" and "ANIMAL-ING." If you cut down a tree in the forest, other trees will feed it to keep it alive. If you physically harm or pleasure an animal, it is Aware of this, correct?

Stars are Awareness in motion and Awareness-ING. A more accurate description is, "STAR-ING." Stars have a well-defined life cycle and have quite an explosive relationship with themselves and the universe. ☺!

This is the universe's paradigm. Your most accurate Self in motion and PURE AWARENESS-BLISS is Being whatever and is the Experiencing and the Happening and the This-ing. This universe is not dead, random, machine-like and mindless, etc. Keep this entire section "parked" in the front of your Awareness when you begin watching SIGHT.

You are already Home.

NOTE

Knowledge is the ability to recall and apply the empirical equation. Awareness is the ability to derive the equation by unveiling an aspect of Reality.

NOTE2

The proverbial rocks are getting more massive. Your most accurate Self in motion is growing up.

NOTE3

Physical and mental athletes believe they attain The Flow. You do not attain what athletes call The Flow*[5]. What is happening is through the intense physical or mental strain the athlete is letting go of the habitual behavior of resistance to The Permanent Now they have been building up and used to since they were around twelve months old. This letting go happens because of the wearing down of the psyche by the prolonged physical or mental effort by the athlete. The athlete does not have any energy left to give to Resistance and therefore the habitual resistance the athlete had become custom to since the athlete was around twelve months old stops. For the briefest of moments, the most fundamental structures of being a human fall away and the athlete gets a small taste of The Permanent Now.

NOTE4

The mind does this usurping within milliseconds of the Happening. Human Awareness is too myopic to be Aware of this usurping. It is amazing. After being Aware of this camouflaging behavior by the human mind, I was on my hands and knees laughing and happy-crying until I could not breathe. ☺

NOTE5

Believing you can attain The Flow perpetuates the illusion that the individual me/ego, the illusory thinker thinking the thoughts and <insert your name here> exist.

games are wonderful
reason and repetition
The Permanent Now

gaming increasing

your transparency of Now

The Permanent Now

GAMES

THEN

Then…

It was a time and place to learn from, remember and forget

It was a time and place to be controlled by

NOW…

It is a story humans create in The Permanent Now

These games help you increase the breadth and depth of your internal self-Awareness. As you play these games from within yourself and with others, Awareness broadens and deepens from within. The increase in Awareness from within increases the potentiality for you to Wake Up in The Permanent Now and drop self-identification with and attachment to Time and all the illusions living in Time.

These games help you move past the conceptualization stage of thought and mental cognition, which is Step Zero and into Awareness and Awakening. These games help you come to the direct experience and realization of The Permanent Now by unveiling THE HERALDS OF NOW and the Awareness within and behind everything.

UNVEILING THE HERALDS OF NOW

Go to a park, library or any other public setting you feel comfortable and quietly sit. Listen with your eyes closed at first and move on playing the game with your eyes open. Listen for THE HERALDS OF NOW. Listen to Friction and Change. Let the sounds of friction and change be the music showing you the way back Home.

Can you hear the library doors opening and closing? Can you hear people whispering? Can you hear sniffles? Can you hear typing? Can you hear a book being put back on a shelf? What style or type of shoe is someone wearing when they walk across the floor? Can you hear someone walking into the library with heels? ☺! Can you hear how tall a person is by the cadence of their stride? Can you hear the different sounds between the turning pages in a book, a magazine and a newspaper? When a person crosses their legs, can you hear if they are wearing denim or another fabric? Can you hear pencil lead moving across paper? Can you hear the air-conditioning or heating fan? Can you hear chirping birds? Can you smell pollen in the air? Can you feel your heartbeat? Can you feel the sun lighting your skin? Can you feel the tension in your face? Can you hear the wind? Can you hear your breath?

Can you hear the wonderfully joyous sound of Stillness and Silence in-between and beneath these sounds? When you settle the human mind by watching it and come to the direct experience and realization of the Stillness and Silence in-between and behind the sounds of friction and change, you are close to Now and directly experiencing and realizing Awareness.

After you become adept at keeping THE HERALDS OF NOW in your Awareness, take the game broader and deeper and keep THE HERALDS OF NOW in your Awareness as you go about your daily activities like having a conversation with someone, while working, driving your car, playing outside, watching television, kissing a loved one, etc.

UNFOLDING PAPER

Awareness is represented by a piece of paper. Awakening is the evolutionary unveiling and unfolding of Awareness and INTEGRATION. Get a blank piece of paper and fold it widthwise into sixteen sections with fifteen folds. Label the top-most folded section of paper PHYSICAL AND MENTAL FORM. Human Awareness is only Aware of the first section of the paper.

Your most accurate Self is Awareness. Awareness holds ALL within it. The first depth of Awareness is Form. After you unfold the piece of paper, you come to the direct experience and realization there are many, many more "things" to Be the Awareness behind. You also understand, through direct experience and realization, **Y**ou are the paper. **Y**ou are the spaciousness, limitlessness and emptiness of Awareness. Form passes through **Y**ou and you are Aware you are not this or that. **Y**ou are the Awareness within and behind this and that.

Lay the folded piece of paper flat on a table with your left hand holding the bottom section which is touching the table and take your right hand and press down the top section of the piece of paper, which is farthest from the table, which has the words PHYSICAL AND MENTAL FORM on it.

The human species is only Aware of the first section of the paper and therefore thinks the species and the individual are the first section of the paper. This is not anywhere near the entire panoramic scene. COME BACK TO NOW and unveil and unfold **Y**ourself.

Now, let go of the paper!

You understand, through direct experience and realization; you are so much more than the first section of the paper.

You have the first section of the paper in your Awareness and Now you are Aware of so much more than the first section. Because of the human species' level of myopic Awareness, you cannot see past the first layer until you fully let go!

Furthermore, there is no end to the paper or to the breadth and depth of Awareness. In fact, the paper is always an ever-receding paper in which Awareness is and is moving toward. ETERNITY AND INFINITY. The evolutionary flow of your most accurate Self is always evolving and INTEGRATING new sections of the paper. When you let go, the paper unfolds Itself and you are Aware **Y**ou were and are, **after all and of course**, the entire paper.

You do not have to go somewhere and do something to have better, smarter or more intricate paper. You do not have to take your paper to a new location to make it better. You cannot unfold your paper through time and make it a process born in time. You cannot give your paper to another physical or mental form and have that thing unfold your paper.

Awakens show you ways to let go of your paper. You must let go and unfold who **You**, **already and of course**, are. Unfolding the paper is INTEGRATION. The human mind thinks everything worth having is hard.

"Nothing worth having is easy to come by." – Unknown

All you need to do is let go of the top section of the paper. The physical game accurately mimics the evolutionary flow. Let go of what you think you are, the first section of the paper, and watch what happens to the paper.

The paper unfolds itself.

You did not do anything. All you "do" is let go of what you think you are. Buddhas show you how to let go. You must be the one letting go of the first section. You must make your call for your pizza! ☺ I understand this might seem scary. **Be noble and brave.** You will not die. You will awaken to The Permanent Now and your most accurate Self! **Total fun!** ☺

AM I HERE, NOW? – #1

While actively listening and watching a conversation unfold; in person, on television, on the radio, at work, in a movie, online, etc., watch and acknowledge how many times people talk about the illusory past and future and do not talk about the Present. After you have mastered the art and skill of observing this behavior outwardly, take your attention within and play the game within yourself.

AM I HERE, NOW? – #2

Count how many times a day you are Aware of thoughts jumping from one state of illusory consciousness to another. Count them and keep a journal. The purpose is to keep a record on how your numbers are tracking.

INTEGRATION

Consciously use the word AND in place of the word BUT. The purpose is to begin your awakening. Part of Awakening is fully accepting and including ALL in The Permanent Now.

Every time you actively listen to a conversation; in person, on television, on the radio, at work, in a movie, online, etc. count how many times the word BUT is used instead of a more accurate term AND. Exchange the word BUT with AND in your conversations and writings. Observe and acknowledge what happens to your mental outlook.

An inaccurate example is, "Awareness isn't hidden. But you can only find it right now. It's only now." An accurate example is, "Awareness isn't hidden and you can only find it right now. It's only now."

Prior to the game, why were events, thoughts, situations, relationships, etc. put into a dual frame of reference? What thing is doing this? What thing lives in a world of duality? After you eliminate the word BUT from your vocabulary and exchanged it with AND, what observations about duality/exclusion and unity, INTEGRATION and inclusion do you have? It is always AND. It is never BUT. INTEGRATION.

NOW PROVIDES WHAT IS NEEDED

The next time you are personally in a situation, watching television, listening to the radio, at work, watching a movie, or are online, etc. and have a question about what is going on with the situation, with the question in your Awareness, slowly count to ten. See what percentage of your questions are answered by the situation, television show, radio, movie, etc. <u>in the first ten seconds</u> of you becoming Aware of wanting to ask about what is going on in the situation, television show, radio, movie, etc. When you are unAware of what to do in life, watch for a little while longer and observe what develops.

COUNTING TO TEN – A TUNING FORK

How much attention do you give attention? Start a stopwatch and lay it aside. Every time you take a breath in and out, start at one and count to ten. This takes ten in-and-out breathes.

When you get to ten go back and count from one to ten, again. Do this for at least an hour. ☺ After you come to the direct experience and realization you left the counting and breathing as your sole focus and are Aware you are somewhere in the illusory reality/realm of past and future consciousness, pick up the stopwatch and see what time has transpired.

Keep doing this until you can go for at least an hour with only your breath and counting in your Awareness. **Total fun.** ☺!

THE PROCESS IS THE GAME

Apply attention to something you find enjoyable, which is physically in your surroundings. Be as mentally still with the object as you can. If you have a challenge becoming mentally still, apply attention to your breathing and the other HERALDS OF NOW and when a HERALD OF NOW becomes all you are Aware of, go back to the object in your Awareness. After you are mentally still and have given your Awareness to the object within your Awareness, describe the happening out loud.

DESCRIBE!

With all five senses, describe whatever forms you are Aware of within your Awareness, after you are mentally still. The point of the game is to go as deep into your Awareness as you can with each of the five senses and describe the way you sense, Now. The point of the game is not to describe more than the other players. This is not a competition. This is a game based in union. Help each other out and use each other as signposts.

WHO WANTS TO PLAY, 'GROWING UP!'?

While in a conversation or relationship with another individual or group, actively take the perspective of the other side of the conversation or relationship.

Take this one step further and do the above for both parties or sides while you are not in and still actively listening to a conversation; in person, on television, on the radio, at work, in a movie, online, etc.

This game moves you through the different breadths and depths of the external identity-centric growth stages of internal human development, from egocentric to ethnocentric to world-centric to universe-centric. In addition to growing up internally, you must grow up externally, as well.

Awakening is
not relatively better
it's absolutely

Awakening now
Awareness is all there is
childish laughter now

AWAKENING

NOW

Then…

Was too small, uneventful and unimportant to even think about

Was nothing more than a vehicle for the next thing to arrive in

NOW…

Is where everything is

Is Reality

Is the archway to PURE AWARENESS-BLISS

One major aspect to spiritual Awakening is lowering the resistance to your inner self you do not want to deal with and **fully** accept. This resistance is the self-identification with and attachment to Time and the illusory reality/realm of past and future consciousness. Therefore, when you lower your resistance to the illusion, you come to the direct experience and realization the illusion is not real and voila, you literally Wake Up, drop Time and unveil The Permanent Now because the illusion/resistance lives in/is illusory Time. Crazy cyclical, huh?

You come to the direct experience and realization of this internal resistance and then lower this internal resistance by watching everything. After lowering this internal resistance, fully accept those aspects of your inner self. Hug The Shadow and come to the direct experience and realization The Shadow is an illusion. Constantly live outside your comfort zones. Did you see this in Chapter Six?

Awakening is unveiling the field of Watching Awareness and the letting go, dropping and the undoing of self-identification with and attachment to Time and all the illusions living in Time.

HUMAN DEVELOPMENT AND AWAKENING

Internal human development is not connected to the physical growth of your body or how long you have lived. Internal human development is about growing, unveiling and integrating more Awareness into you*. Get out of your comfort zones and then constantly stay outside your comfort zones. This can greatly help your awakening.

Internal growth and Awakening is about lowering the resistance you have towards aspects of your inner self (getting out of your comfort zones) and then hugging those resistances to your inner self (embracing everything outside your comfort zones). **Lower resistance. Hug The Shadow.** Come to the direct experience and realization The Shadow, Time, Suffering and Fear, among other things are illusory.

Human Awareness and what most humans label consciousness has four fundamental breadths and depths and areas of growth, unveiling and integration. For this section only, the label CONSCIOUSNESS is used instead of Awareness because the label CONSCIOUSNESS is more ubiquitous than the label Awareness. Consciousness and Awareness are synonyms unless when the label CONSCIOUSNESS is used for thought consciousness.

The enveloping and increasing breadths and depths of consciousness growth, unveiling and integration are Persona, Ego, Centaur and Unity. You define who you are and how you relate to this universe by the breadth and depth of your consciousness.

Persona consciousness is the consciousness of young people, around ages one to seven. Everyone starts at the same place. Around twelve months old, people begin self-identifying with and attaching to Time and all the illusions living in Time. Some people choose to stay in their comfort zones and do not internally grow, unveil and integrate the enveloping and increasing breadths and depths of consciousness.

The Persona resists The Shadow and internal growth, unveiling and integration is halted. Your internal issues and symptoms stay around. When the Persona lowers resistance to its internal issues and then accepts The Shadow, internal growth, unveiling and integration continue. Most people internally grow, unveil and integrate consciousness a little, mostly because society demands it. These humans internally grow, unveil and integrate the breadths and depths of their consciousness from Persona to Ego.

Ego consciousness is the current myopic breadth and depth of the vast majority of people. You agree the vast majority of people "have an ego" and relate to the universe accordingly, correct? Most people stop their internal growth, unveiling and integration at this breadth and depth of consciousness. This usually happens because of traumatic life events or because society's structure in the early twenty-first century rewards this level of human development*[2]. These are two of the biggest reasons most people stay in this comfort zone and do not internally grow, unveil and integrate the enveloping and increasing breadths and depths of consciousness.

The Ego resists The Shadow and internal growth, unveiling and integration stop. Your internal issues and symptoms stay around. Stop moving back and forth from one illusory future thought to an illusory past thought and vice versa. When the Ego lowers resistance to its internal issues and then accepts The Shadow, internal growth, unveiling and integration continue. Lower your resistance to your internal issues and accept The Shadow and continue your internal growth, unveiling and integration of the enveloping and increasing breadths and depths of consciousness.

Very rarely, some people actively stay outside their comfort zones constantly enough to integrate and unify their body and mind. These humans internally grow, unveil and integrate the breadths and depths of consciousness from Ego to Centaur. The Centaur label is used to represent the mythical character of a unified human and horse. This image represents the integration and unification of mind and body. Most of these people stay in their comfort zones and do not internally grow, unveil and integrate the enveloping and increasing breadths and depths of consciousness.

Centaurs resist The Permanent Now creating pathologies. Watch the internal mental chatter and the voice in your head. This mental chatter creates disturbances in your psyche. These disturbances create pathologies. Remember the ulcerative colitis in Chapter Six? When the Centaur lowers resistance to its internal issues and then accepts The

Shadow, internal growth, unveiling and integration continues. Causeless Joy is close. ☺

As a species of around one hundred and eight billion people, several hundred to a thousand-ish were **noble and brave** and kept internally growing, unveiling and integrating. We completely grew up, internally developed, evolved and expanded the breadths and depths of our consciousness and unveiled Unity Consciousness and the innate buddhahood nature and literally Woke Up to the natural state of existence, an Awaken.

Internal growth happens in the perceived troughs and valleys of life not at the crests and peaks. Fully accept the perceived troughs and valleys of life as fundamental for your internal growth, unveiling and integration. The crests and peaks of life are times to rest, recuperate, recover and appreciate. ☺ Engage Change. Your most accurate Self is SO AMAZING!

Awakens are extremely, extremely, extremely…extremely rare. We need not be. Everyone is already a sleeping buddha. Awakens are the only ones Aware of this.

Your oldest and most constant resistance is your resistance to Reality, The Permanent Now. There is only The Permanent Now. Darkness is only driven out by The Light of Awareness.

When you self-identify with and attach to Time and all the illusions living in Time, your myopic Awareness is hypnotized and resists The Permanent Now. Stop resisting The Permanent Now and unveil your **already and of course** Unity consciousness.

Unity Consciousness is everyone's natural and underlying state of consciousness. Unity Consciousness is the consciousness which is the Within Ness and Behind Ness of everything, forever. Around twelve months old, **You** begin self-identifying with and attaching to Time and all the illusions living in Time and cover up the ultimate breadth and depth of consciousness by resisting The Permanent Now. This resistance layers these illusions on **You** and covers, veils and masks The Permanent Now. This resistance blocks the Light of Awareness and your most accurate Self.

You cannot <u>attain</u> Unity Consciousness. How can you attain your most accurate Self? You must <u>unveil</u> your most accurate Self. This happens by integrating all the above breadths and depths of consciousness; Persona, Ego and Centaur. This can happen slowly throughout life or extremely quickly with a sudden Awakening. The breadths and depths of Awareness show me "slow and steady" <u>is a great catalyst</u> for increasing the probability, possibility and potentiality of your awakening.

The pain you associate with internal growth and The Shadow is not real. I am Aware you think the pain is real. **Be noble and brave.** By Watching, push through, past and out of the illusory pain you feel inside and come to the direct experience and realization the pain keeping you in your comfort zones is not real. The pain you associate with internal growth and The Shadow is not real. Do you think fifty-plus centuries of repetitious guidance is enough repetition to take your first step? **Continuously with a smile. Do not stop. Do not expect.**

THE SEARCH FOR SPIRITUAL ENLIGHTENMENT

The mind lives in the illusory reality/realm of linear-ness. You think you must do this and then that to reach an objective. This is accurate from the perspective of thought, mental cognition and conceptualization. Humans think spiritual enlightenment is a search because of all the experiences humans have with reaching objectives, goals and accomplishments is perceived as linear. Direct experience and realization are instantaneous, non-linear and without Time. Thought is linear and exists in Time.

Repetitiously COMING BACK TO NOW is like peeling back layers of inaccuracy until you unveil CLARITY and ACCURACY. Inaccuracy is self-identification with and attachment to Time and all the illusions living in Time. CLARITY and ACCURACY are The Permanent Now.

The Paradox of Doing and Not Doing

You cannot do anything to attain spiritual Awakening and enlightenment. How can you <u>do</u> something to attain That which you **already and of course** are? Trying to do something moves you out of The Permanent Now. Not trying to do something is still a doing just the other side of the coin.

Therefore, if you cannot do anything and trying to not do anything is still another type of doing, how does one spiritually Awaken and "become enlightened?"

A key is understanding you are constantly resisting The Permanent Now and aspects of your inner self with your self-identification with and attachment to Time and all the illusions living in Time.

You must lower your resistance to The Permanent Now and all the aspects of your inner self. After you lower this resistance to The Permanent Now and all the aspects of your inner self, you must hug the resistance to those aspects of your inner self. You do all of this by watching. You do all of this by being your most accurate Self, which is Watching Awareness. Resistance is turning away from The Permanent Now, not actively engaging as Watching Awareness and not being your most accurate Self.

This universe and your life is not a test or a challenge! Your most accurate Self is PURE Joy, Stillness and Love. You need not compete, conquer or win at anything to live an engaged, full and wondrous life. Lower resistance. Hug The Shadow. Lowering resistance and hugging The Shadow are not doings. They are increasing the breadth and depth of internal self-Awareness.

GOOD THOUGHTS AND BAD THOUGHTS

Good thoughts will not overpower and overcome bad thoughts. All thoughts are getting "manufactured" in the same "manufacturing plant" and your goal is to "walk outside" the manufacturing plant and look back and realize "the manufacturing plant" is not real.

You must fully accept your bad thoughts. Do not judge yourself for having bad thoughts in your Awareness. Fully accept and acknowledge all thought by watching. Then watch them lose their intensity, substantiality, compulsion and importance and unveil their illusoriness. Then your self-identification with and attachment to them lessens.

THE EMPTY FIELD ANALOGY

Picture a vast, empty and infinitely wide-open field with the word AWARENESS painted on the grass. You are the empty field. There are two types of people on

> **You**. One group is cheering and the other group is booing.
>
> The individual people represent thoughts. One group is good thought. The other group is bad thought. The field is full of people who come and go. Thoughts always come and go.
>
> Watch the people on the field. Be the vast, empty and infinitely wide-openness of the field. Be **You**. **You** neither cheer nor boo any of the people. **You** are not a fan. **You** are the empty field of Watching Awareness.

To be spiritual does not mean to have no bad thoughts. This perspective keeps you self-identified with and attached to Time, all the illusions living in Time and in the Illusion of Duality and Relativeness. Holding this perspective keeps you fighting the fighter. This perspective keeps resistance to The Permanent Now in place.

To be spiritual does not mean being perfect. To be spiritual means being whole. To be whole is becoming Aware of your resistance to aspects of your inner self, lowering that resistance to those aspects of your inner self and then hugging The Shadow. When you lower resistance to The

Shadow, you release its intensity, substantiality, compulsion and importance and unveil its illusoriness. When you resist The Shadow, you give the illusion intensity, substantiality and importance. **Be noble and brave. Do not stop. Do not expect.**

When all the above happens, you integrate those aspects of your walled-off Awareness and psyche by lowering resistance and hugging The Shadow. You are lowering your walls, barriers and divisions and integrating those walled-off areas of your psyche into **You**.

The Permanent Now has no thoughts to agree with, no beliefs to adhere to and no doings to get done. These things are not what Waking Up is. Waking Up starts with constant watching, observing and accepting of all things created from within and without.

"Out beyond ideas of wrongdoing and rightdoing,
there is a field. I'll meet you there." – Rumi

Awakening is not about working really hard, grasping for and then attaining enlightenment. You must let go of your spiritually enlightened ego trip. Awakening is not a process. How could there be a process to get you to where **You** already live, The Permanent Now? You must watch what is being created right Here, right Now. When you are resting as Watching Awareness, you come to the direct experience and realization; you are at the beginning of the individual me/ego's end. How much sincerity, attention and repetition you give within and behind dictates how quickly you begin your awakening.

You will rub the proverbial sleep from your eyes, yawn, stretch out your arms and smile at the world you have seen for your entire life and strangely see this wondrous place for the very first time! The direct experience and realization is wonderful beyond words and comprehension. ☺

After you literally Wake Up, Life starts freely living through you and you have everything you need. This universe provides what it needs for you and not necessarily what the human mind wants. Why would your most accurate Self create this entire universe for you to Wake Up in and unveil who **Y**ou are, all the while beating you down and making your existence in **Y**our creation a complete nightmare and hell? PURE AWARENESS-BLISS does not do this. The mind does this.

AWAKENING – THE NEXT EVOLUTIONARY STEP

Self-identification with and attachment to Time and all the illusions living in Time is like the human tailbone or the gills a human has early in its developing stages of life. They are relics of eras long gone. The human mind thinks Evolution is what physically happens to a life form to make it a new species. This is accurate and not the entire story.

The physical-ness of humans happened on this planet with this form of Awareness in motion labeled the human form. The mental-ness of evolution and the nervous system of life forms have been developing along a parallel path with the physical-ness of evolution.

A single-celled organism has a less developed nervous system than a thirty-two-trillion-celled organism. The nervous system is the beginnings of mental-ness within the INTEGRATION and evolution of LIFE. Over two-hundred thousand years ago, the major mental-ness on Earth evolved into homo sapiens.

Thought evolved from, "How can I get out of this tree, onto the grasslands where food and safety are more plentiful, into an environment which is not crowded with competition and do all of this without dying?" to all the manifestations we are Aware of today. Thought is the operating system of humans. Thought runs humans. Human Awareness evolved from a radar-like scanning system used to detect differences, changes and anomalies in the environment and the tool which creates other tools and eventually distorted, transformed and contorted into the illusory individual me/ego.

Awakening is experiencing LIFE directly and not through the filter of Time and all the illusions living in Time.

Glasses Analogy

You are looking through a pair of glasses ever since you were around twelve months old. The glasses are Time and Thought. All things have structure and content. The frames or the structure of the glasses are the illusory reality/realm of past and future consciousness. The lenses and specifically the prescription of the lenses and the way the lenses are curved and more accurately the way the lenses bend The Permanent Now into what the lenses want The Permanent Now to look like is the content of the glasses.

The prescription of the lenses or how you perceive Reality is unique to each individual person. Each person has their own illusory style of past and future consciousness, i.e. their specific glasses' prescription. Therefore, there are approximately seven-and-a-half billion different human realities on this planet. Any wondering why there is so much conflict and suffering on this planet?

> Begin your awakening by removing your glasses and seeing LIFE, Now, not LIFE distorted, transformed and contorted through Time and the illusory reality/realm of past and future consciousness.

By watching everything, self-identification with and attachment to Time and all the illusions living in Time eventually ends.

After this happens, the human mind completely rests and Awareness shines through and you are Aware and are Aware **Y**ou are Awareness. ☺! As you continue resting the human mind by watching **it**, Awareness increases in breadth and depth. When you come to the direct experience and realization Now is all there is, you have Awakened in The Permanent Now. ☺

No one can and no one has to verify your awakening. You are Awake or you are not Awake. You will most definitely be Aware of it. ☺

As you begin your awakening, you feel parts of the body from a new breadth, depth and perspective. You also come to the direct experience and realization of so many more innate nesses of this universe than the human mind could ever think. How do you think The Permanent Now was written? ☺!

VAULT CRACKING ANALOGY

Perceiving spiritual Awakening is like cracking into a huge bank vault is inaccurate. The human mind cannot and therefore does not step back and see what most accurately is. There is no vault.

By watching everything, actively move back from the vault's rotary dial and see there are no walls to the safe and there is no rotary dial. The human mind thinks it must crack into the safe and get the riches. You cannot become enlightened. You already are. Drop the search. Drop the safe's rotary dial. Stop thinking about the clicks on the rotary dial and Be.

AWAKENING AND WAKING UP

The universe's flow is one-way. As soon as someone Wakes Up, they are permanently Awake. This is accurate and not the entire story. Waking Up happens Now, in one moment.

Unless your awakening is instantaneous, Awakening is like coming out of a dream. It takes consistency and repetition in The Permanent Now. The breadth and depth of your awakening and Awareness depend on the level of active and internal nurturing of Watching Awareness from within. Awakening is ongoing and dynamic. Awakening is not static and a one-time deal. Waking Up is a one-time deal.

Awakening is like a snowball rolling down a mountain. At first, it might seem challenging to start the snowball rolling down the mountain. After a while, the snowball has more than enough inertia to roll down the entire mountain on its own. The same can happen in you.

Awakening is like a child learning to walk. At first, walking instead of !crawling on the ground and in the dirt! seems to take a lot of effort and return very little. After a while, the initial amount of effort is looked back on as inconsequential and almost imperceivably small. Because internal attention increases in breadth and depth so quickly, after a while, you almost forget how you could have ever thought the beginning was ever difficult. Not because Now has so much more difficulty. Because Now, you realize there is no difficulty. The same can happen in you.

INTENSE SITUATIONS

Potential opportunities for Awakening is not resisting mentally intense situations. Humans habitually train themselves to turn away from mentally intense situations. Do not turn away! Stay! Turn into them! Fully accept them!

This can be a very accurate opportunity for Waking Up. Why turn into them? So, you can come to the direct experience and realization that self-identification with and attachment to Time and all the illusions living in Time is an illusion and not accurately Real. ☺ It is an awesome direct experience and realization to have. **Total fun!**

DRIVING ON ICE

When you drive on ice and you lose control of the steering, do you turn your steering wheel away from the concern, the slide? No, you do not. The only accurate way out of the situation is to turn into the slide. Turn into your intense thoughts. If they are intense enough and you fully turn into them and fully accept them, the illusory self-identification with and attachment to Time and the illusory thinker thinking the thoughts burn themselves up! ☺

You are reading The Permanent Now because you want something different. You got to this page because you are tired of doing the same thing and not getting out of your suffering. Do something different and turn into those thoughts, feelings, emotions and beliefs! The only Real thing is The Permanent Now and your most accurate Self.

Step Zero and Beyond

Understanding and conceptualizing signposts is Step Zero. After Step Zero, you understand signposts and where signposts are pointing. Now go to Step One, listening for The Heralds of Now. Then move to Step Two, repetitiously Coming Back To Now and through repetition stay Here, Now and unveil The Permanent Now. Step Three, use The Permanent Now as the archway and lighthouse to meet your most accurate Self, Pure Awareness-Bliss - The Source creat<u>ing</u> this universe.

You can look at Awakening this way and use these steps. Understanding and conceptualizing signposts is Step Zero. Step One, actively lower resistance to aspects of your inner self. Step Two, accept those aspects of your inner self. Step Three, move through, past and out of the illusory reality/realm of Time and past and future consciousness and literally Wake Up in The Permanent Now.

Boredom

When you are close to The Permanent Now, boredom <u>parks</u> in your Awareness. When you are Aware of boredom, you are exactly where you are choosing to be! Watch boredom come into your Watching Awareness and then accept boredom fully and watch it pass out of **You**. Remember; non-judgment, non-resistance, non-attachment and full acceptance to All which passes through **You**. The more you self-identify with and give attachment to a thing the longer that thing will stay in your Awareness.

"What you resist, persists." – Carl Jung

What is not interesting to a thing that enjoys grinding away at other things within its focus to find the ever-elusive Happiness and Connection? NOthing is not interesting. Boredom is an enemy of the human mind. The human mind will do anything to keep boredom at bay. The human mind eats, drinks and inhales poisons rather than just sitting still and Being. Find out where boredom comes. What is more boring to resistance than Peace? What is more unusual, uncomfortable and unnerving to an entity, which is constantly moving and searching for accurate Peace? STILLNESS! Reality is amazing!! It is so simple and so close to all humans.

GRACE

The breadth of The Permanent Now is CLARITY and horizontal. The depth of The Permanent Now is ACCURACY and vertical. There is a variable to Awakening labeled Grace. Grace is the unknown factor helping you Awaken. Therefore, all these spaces, letters, words, sentences, sections and chapters are only signposts. The gap in CLARITY and ACCURACY between where the signpost ends and where you need to Be is Awareness. My direct experience and realization shows me Grace is the confidence you have in LIFE, the universe and **Y**ourself. Stay open and do not internally close off for any reason.

Your most accurate Self is creating this entire universe, so you can awaken to your most accurate Self and integrate beyond. ☺ You are wonderful and worthy. You are playing hide and seek with your most accurate Self. The universe is an evolving integration of manifested Awareness. Keep this in the foreground of your Watching Awareness.

HEAVEN, JANNAH/FIRDAUS, YOU, ETC.

Heaven is REAL. Heaven, another label for your most accurate Self, is more real than this universe. This universe will...eventually...end. Your most accurate Self has no beginning and therefore no end. An aspect of your most accurate Self is Eternity and Infinity*[3]. After you finish what you call "your life," you go back being your most accurate Self. You go back being The Source constantly creating this universe. There is not your most accurate Self in Heaven. There is only **Y**ou.

THE SHADOW

The Shadow is an illusion resulting from resisting The Permanent Now. When you resist The Permanent Now, you turn away from, conceal and veil The Light of Awareness, which always and only lives in The Permanent Now. Therefore, you "fall" into illusory darkness and self-identify with and attach to the illusory Shadow. Your resistances are the illusory walls, barriers and divisions in your psyche. Your resistances are the unresolved past and future issues you bury deep in the illusory reality/realm of Time and past and future consciousness.

End your resistance to The Permanent Now, unveil The Light of Awareness, which always and only lives in accurate Reality and directly experience and realize The Shadow is an illusion. Time, Fear and mental suffering are illusions. You end this resistance to The Permanent Now by watching everything, especially "the things" on the inside of you.

WAVES OF STILLNESS

When you begin Awakening and unveiling your most accurate Self, you feel a difference from within. The most accurate way to describe this, and it is still not accurate, is a wave of energy or Stillness envelops you from within. This direct experience and realization may startle you. What you think you are has never experienced this Happening before. You will probably "ride the wave" of Stillness for a very short period. This is fine. Do not try to "ride the wave" of Stillness longer. Allow it to be. Do not chase the wave. The wave comes back. The wave is an aspect and hue of your most accurate Self. Sooner or later you come to the direct experience and realization you are the entire ocean and not just "the wave."

TIMEPIECES

If you are sincere about Awakening, cover up and put away all timepieces like; watches, car clocks, computer clocks, microwave clocks, stove clocks, phone clocks, etc. Use your phone alarm for all your appointments. Humans and their timepieces??? Eventually, you come to the direct experience and realization The Flow is.

You are already Home.

CHALLENGES WITH AWAKENING

A misperception toward Awakening is misunderstanding the lack of internal sincerity, attention and repetition needed. Early on, there is likely to be a perceived challenge of staying attentive to Now. It takes effort and energy to cover up, hide from and resist The Permanent Now and PURE AWARENESS. You have spent this great amount of effort and energy since you were around twelve months old. You are used to the amount of effort used as the mind. It takes repetition to become comfortable with the lessening of this great amount of effort used as the mind. It takes no effort at all to Be in The Permanent Now.

Some obstacles for Awakening are; self-induced perceived comfort – people attach to suffering, a lack of motivation – people are attached to suffering, the subject is not spoken about enough – most people are unAware of being unAware and the lack of sincere, active, consistent and internal nurturing of Awareness from within for one's internal state.

Awakening is like waking up in your bed. If you want to Wake Up quicker, let as much **Light** shine on you as you feel comfortable. The more Awareness you INTEGRATE into your life, the more Awareness grows within you. ☺!

PARADOX OF COMMUNICATION

Because the topics an Awaken speaks on are not out there in Space, Time and Form, most humans do not understand, believe or trust buddhas*4. An Awaken points you within, which is not of Space, Time and Form all the while talking with someone who thinks they are of Space, Time and Form.

Early Awakens are not a god or the son of god. Pedestalizing or worshiping any buddha, especially historically popular Awakens, keeps you in the reality/realm of Relativeness and keeps you in the conceptualization stage*5. Do not give your authority away.

NOTE

People who are more internally developed, grown-up and mature are more Aware, correct? Are people who judge other people based on skin color, gender, sexual orientation, social-economic status, intelligence, religion, etc. highly Aware? Are internally developed, grown-up and mature adults who live outside their comfort zones through their entire lives more Aware than adults who experienced no challenges in life and therefore left none of their myopic and self-centered comfort zones?

Study Maslow's Hierarchy Pyramid. What is at the very tip-top of the pyramid*[6]? Self-actualization is the scientific and clinical label for spiritual Awakening and enlightenment.

NOTE2

Humans build mental walls, barriers and divisions which internally separate them from ever experiencing anything outside their comfort zones. Most people do not want to experience the change associated with a traumatic life event. This walling-off behavior halts internal growth. What personal traumatic life events convinced you to build walls, barriers and divisions, which are separating you from new positive experiences of growth, unveiling and integration and keeping you in your comfort zones? Unveil your inalienable birthright to be Aware of your most accurate Self and live your most accurate life? Watch your walling-off behavior. This is resistance to The Permanent Now. Stay outside your comfort zones. **Be noble and brave.**

NOTE3

When your Awareness integrates back into **REAL LIFE** and you temporarily Wake Up out of the dream of this universe and come to the direct experience and realization of your most accurate Self, you come to the direct experience and realization of Eternity and Infinity. Eternity and Infinity are aspects and hues of your most accurate Self. The direct experience and realization of Eternity and Infinity is beyond words and comprehension. **Total fun!** ☺

NOTE4

Parallel the last lesson of Plato's allegorical tale, *The Cave.*

NOTE5

Historically, a person's last name was a descriptor of what (s)he did. Jane Carpenter was Jane that did carpentry. John Cooke was John that cooked food. The last name Christ is Greek for Christos*[7]. Christos is a Greek pronoun or title meaning "the anointed one." "The anointed one" is interchangeable with the label MESSIAH which is a Hebrew and Aramaic label meaning "the one who relieves suffering." All life forms on Earth can provide guidance to humans and help humans out of their suffering. All life on Earth are messiahs for the human species. Buddhas are the only life forms accurately communicating; verbally and via written word with humans on how to unveil The Permanent Now and spiritually Awaken.

Chisel away all the superlative meanings of the pronoun or title Christos and messiah and you get "the Awakened one or the enlightened one." For over fifty centuries, buddhas have been coming and going in every culture. Stop pedestalizing buddhas, especially historically popular buddhas. Why would you pedestalize another version of your most accurate Self?

NOTE6

What is on top of the tip-top of Maslow's hierarchy? Providing exceptionally accurate guidance to people for their own Self-actualization. ☺!

NOTE7

The Romance languages evolved out of Latin. Latin evolved out of the Etruscan and Greek alphabets. The Greek language evolved out of Sanskrit. Sanskrit is the mother of western languages.

when chaos abounds
stay sincere and attentive
Watching is the key

seekers focus on
attaining buddhahood, no!
Watching is the key

WATCHING AWARENESS

HEAVEN

Then…

A place good people went after death

A place for people who believed certain thoughts

NOW…

Heaven can awaken within you

Heaven is **You, after all and of course**

Watching Awareness has four fundamental pillars, aspects and hues; Non-judgment, Non-resistance, Non-attachment and full Acceptance. Use the following to COME BACK TO NOW, lower resistance to your inner self, hug The Shadow and with repetition stay Here, Now and unveil The Permanent Now.

NON-JUDGMENT

With non-judgment in the Here and Now, there is no mental labeling of What Is. Everything in this universe is manifested Awareness. Why would you judge What Is? Why would you judge **Y**ourself? Why would you judge who **Y**ou are in another and an other form? Why would you judge something, which has already happened or has not happened? It Is What It Is.

Getting What Is to Here and Now happen previously and previously is not Here, Now. **Watch.**

Do you know everything? ☺ Are you Aware of Everything? What in you is so afraid or arrogant that it needs, wants or has all the answers? Now is the only moment this universe gives anyone and, in this moment, What Is already is What Is.

Non-judgment helps you COME BACK TO NOW and rest Here. Non-judgment does not affix an anchor of correctness and truth to an idea or perspective. Judgment does this. Non-judgment keeps you out of the illusory reality/realm of Relativeness. Non-judgment allows things to come and go. LIFE has a fluidness and flow to it. Do not resist this fluidness and The Flow.

Judgment stops this fluidness and The Flow. Judgment shifts What Is into a thing with an absoluteness within the reality/realm of the human mind. Absoluteness is not helpful to Awakening. Non-judgment allows things to exist in The Permanent Now. Non-judgment keeps you out of the illusory reality/realm of past and future consciousness.

Linguistically and mentally labeling things initiates judgment. Judgment is one of the initializers of Time and self-identification with and attachment to Thought.

Words are labels. Limit and with repetition altogether stop using words in your mental Awareness. Accept What Is for What It Is. There is no use for mental labels when Awakening is the aim. Non-judgment allows for a more accurate sense of non-resistance.

NON-RESISTANCE

Why resist What Is? It already is the way it is. Resisting What Is, is resisting LIFE and The Permanent Now. Resisting What Is, is the beginning of mental insanity and self-identification with and attachment to Time and all the illusions living in Time.

You can consciously change What Is. To change What Is to whatever, you must fully and authentically accept What Is. Non-resistance is being malleable, flexible and ever-changing. Be the young nubile sapling and not the cracked-in-half old tree, which never flexed and bent during stormy times.

Be as intellectually honest and internally transparent to yourself as you can.

The importance of non-resistance is understanding The Permanent Now is **always** changing. An Awaken is Aware of this fundamental universal principle and is in step with The Flow of LIFE and the ever-changing Permanent Now. Non-resistance allows for a more accurate sense of non-attachment.

NON-ATTACHMENT

Non-attachment is the pillar, aspect and hue of Watching Awareness where you are Aware all things are in a constant state of change. Do you truly, accurately and sincerely want to COME BACK to your natural state of existence, unveil your accurate sanity and push through, burn up and shine Awareness on your current breadth and depth of insanity?

How can you stay attached to that which is in constant change? It is not possible to stay attached to that which is in constant change and yet humans try for their entire life*. Read the definition of Insanity, right now. LIFE is PURE AWARENESS-BLISS in motion. LIFE is INTEGRATION. LIFE is Change. All things born in Space, Time and Form change and eventually leave this universe.

This universe is INTEGRATIVE CHANGE.

Do you want to ease your suffering? Apply attention to the process of whatever you are doing, which is always in The Permanent Now and not the illusory outcome which lives in the illusory reality/realm of future consciousness and watch the universe take care of Itself. ☺! Actively hand over and give control to your most accurate Self and unveil you already have the control humans so desperately grasp for. Let go and let your most accurate Self…Be.

Outcomes live in the illusory reality/realm of future consciousness. Do not let an illusory outcome bind, entrap and imprison You. In The Permanent Now, there is no outcome. There is only This. Stay Present and fulfill This. Fulfill this Moment! Do whatever this Moment asks of you and watch! Do not attach to non-attachment.

It is your self-identification with and attachment to Time and Thought which validates and gives substantiality to your suffering. When there is no attachment, there are no concerns. How do you drop attachment? Watch everything and unveil suffering's illusory ness. Non-attachment allows for a greater sense of The Permanent Now and full acceptance.

FULL ACCEPTANCE

Full acceptance is innate to the sutra, It is What It Is. The seed of non-attachment blossoms into full acceptance. Full acceptance grows into Watching Awareness. If you do not fully accept What Is, you turn away from What Is and turn toward mental insanity, which is self-identification with and attachment to the illusory reality/realm of past and future consciousness and resistance to The Permanent Now.

Conversations you have within yourself and with others about illusory past and future events do not change What Is. When you fully accept What Is, you release resistance, conflict and suffering from within. Instead of creating opinions and thoughts about illusory past and future events in your life, fully accept The Permanent Now.

Fully accepting the less integrated Now and internal personal issues releases their grasp on your psyche. This release makes it exceedingly less challenging for you to Be, Here, Now. If you cannot accept What Is, accept that you cannot accept What Is. This acceptance of not accepting acceptance begins releasing you from what is within your myopic Awareness.

In the beginning, always hold five cards in your front pocket. On the back of the five cards write; I am Here Now, Non-resistance, Non-attachment, Non-judgment, Full Acceptance.

There is no reason to accept any physical or mental pain from anyone, especially your mind.

WATCHING

By Watching, dis-identify with and lessen the attachment to Time and all the illusions living in Time. Watching everything brings Watching Awareness to the forefront and your self-identification with and attachment to Time and all the illusions living in Time lessens and eventually burns up.

Are you Aware of the sound your voice makes? What about your physical presence in a room? What other personal physical creations are you unAware of? When will you acknowledge the Awareness within and behind these things? Whenever that is, it will always be Now.

!NOT MINDFULNESS!

Watching Awareness is not labeled mindfulness! This inaccuracy shows how deeply humans self-identify with, attach to and myopically focus on the mind. Watching Awareness is not full-of-mind-ness! Watching Awareness is the exact opposite of full-of-mind-ness!

Do not do mindfulness.

You are not "searching for stillness." Stillness is a by-product of Watching.

You must Watch.

NOTE

Trying to hold That which is in constant change is like trying to find Heaven anywhere other than in Reality, The Permanent Now. It is impossible…and…yet!…humans have been trying for over two-hundred thousand years.

buddhas watch the world
buddhas are neither attached
nor detached, Watching

THE PERMANENT NOW

The Permanent Now speaks with more breadth
and depth than Thought could ever think.

Self-identification with and attachment to Time and the illusory reality/realm of past and future consciousness is happening in The Permanent Now.

You cannot think about the illusory past in the past. **Y**ou do not live in the past. The "past" never existed. The story called "the past" lives in The Permanent Now. It is only a story created with the illusion of Time. **Have you ever experienced the past?** How could you have ever accurately lived in an illusion???

You cannot think about the illusory future in the future. **Y**ou do not live in the future. The "future" will never exist. The story called "the future" lives in The Permanent Now. It is only a story created with the illusion of Time. **Have**

you ever experienced the future? How will you ever accurately live in an illusion???

You live in The Permanent Now. Stop resisting Reality and Be Here, Now.

After around twelve months old, individually and as a species, humans have no direct experience and realization of The Permanent Now.

THE HERALDS OF NOW

THE HERALDS OF NOW make up the Archway of The Permanent Now. Through watching everything, have your myopic Awareness broaden and deepen and have It leave the illusory reality/realm of past and future consciousness and expand into the realm of Sound and beyond. What is the farthest sound you can hear right now? Can you read these sentences and actively listen to those distant sounds, concurrently? This shows you a brief glimpse into the level of attention you give Sincerity, Attention and Watching Awareness.

You might have read or heard about the doorway or gateway to Now. A door and gate conjure images of barriers like; a doorknob, a keyhole, a key and a lock. All these potential images are images of restriction. The Permanent Now is not restricted by anyone or for any individual or group. How can Reality be restricted by anyone or for anyone? The label, the doorway or gateway to The Permanent Now, is less accurate than The Archway of The Permanent Now.

THE HERALDS OF NOW make up the Archway. THE HERALDS OF NOW sing their specific song reminding you where Now is. Through song, they remind you to COME BACK to your most accurate home. They are lighthouses to be unveiled after a voyage out into the sea of Time and the illusory reality/realm of past and future consciousness. Through song, THE HERALDS OF NOW light the way back to Reality, The Permanent Now.

Quiet the human mind by becoming Aware of THE HERALDS of Now. Some HERALDS are; chirping crickets, singing cicadas, the hum of fluorescent lights at work, the hum of tires on the road, singing birds, a babbling brook, the tenor, cadence and subtle inflections of the voice you listen to Now, a slight wind across your ears, the choreographed dance of leaves on a tree by the slow-moving wind, the changing rainbow-colored hues of a sunrise and sunset, the dance of a spider's web on the wind's current, dry leaves rustling along concrete, pollen in the air, the savoriness of food and your body's ever-present song, the song of breath.

When you unveil THE HERALDS, you are close to the Archway of The Permanent Now. Stay with THE

HERALDS. **You** are this Watching Awareness. You cannot grasp for Awareness. You cannot grasp for **Y**ourself. **You** are not any thing. **Y**ou are the field of Watching Awareness holding every thing within **Y**ourself. Let go, slip in and expand into ALL. You are mentally stepping back from Time and the illusory reality/realm of past and future consciousness and becoming Aware of all things. **Y**ou are stepping back from Time and the human mind and being Aware of What Is. **Y**ou are expanding your current breadth and depth of Awareness. Read The Building You Think You Are Analogy again.

When you are listening, feeling, seeing, tasting and touching THE HERALDS OF NOW for long enough, you realize LIFE'S soundtrack is a very nice soundtrack.

The Permanent Now, not much to talk
about and a lot to experience.

THE PERMANENT NOW IS THE EVOLVING STAGE

Motion only exists in The Permanent Now. Reality is Integrative Change in The Permanent Now.

THE PERMANENT NOW

- Almost fourteen billion years ago, this universe was manifested from NOthing-ness. STILLNESS dreams Motion. With **sheer exuberance**, your most accurate

Self begins The Dream of Motion and Integrative Change.

- **BANG!**
- A lot of cooling happens. ☺
- The gravitational pull of the swirling gas in the early universe created one entire generation of stars. The stars' lives were around five billion years.
- Our sun is a second or third-generation star in the Milky Way Galaxy.
- Our sun is approximately five billion years old and will be around for approximately another five billion years.
- A nearby star explodes into a supernova and the iron created in that star and from its supernova crosses into our sun's gravity well and becomes the Earth's core. You live on a sliver of a supernova.
- A lot more cooling happens.
- Earth continues revolving around the Sun and through accretion, gathers rocks, minerals and elements.
- A huge Mars-sized planet collides with Earth.
    - The new Earth's iron core increases from the union of both the previous planets' cores.
    - The Moon forms.
- After this integration, two <u>synergistic</u> events occur.
    - The newly formed Earth's axis tilts 23.5 degrees, allowing for <u>seasons</u>.
    - The Earth settles in the Goldie Locks Orbital Zone around the Sun. This zone is neither too hot nor too cold for Life to begin. It is juuust right.

- The newly formed iron core has two layers to it. The center core is solid iron. The outer core is molten iron and rotates around the inner solid core. This dynamic relationship turns the rotational energy into electromagnetic energy and a synergistic outcome is the magnetic shield around Earth and a different type and style of protective atmosphere for all Earthlings to enjoy.
  - Without Earth's magnetic shield, Earth's atmosphere and life on Earth would not exist for long. Due to the Sun's solar flare and coronal mass ejections activity, Earth would end up like Mars – a dead planet.
- The gravitational stability between the Earth and the Moon slows Earth's rotational orbit down on the x, y and z-axes. Day-night cycle expands.
  - This gravitationally stabilizing relationship between Earth and the Moon stopped Earth from wobbling and a synergistic outcome is the potentiality for life to exist on this planet for extended periods of time.
- Earth creates life. Relatively recently, Antarctica creates global-level wind and water currents. Antarctica's value is enormous to all current life on Earth*.
- The DNA of physical life is not a replica of its parents. It is a union of both. This INTEGRATION creates differences. Over time, these differences are the physical synergistic evolution of all life on this planet.

Recapping INTEGRATION within this part of the universe; Quarks, then Hydrogen, etc., then Iron, then supernovas, etc., then amino acids, then peptides and proteins, etc., then a single-celled organism, then a multi-celled organism, then a plant, then an invertebrate, then a vertebrate, etc., then your parents meet, etc., then you, etc. Now you are reading this sentence. INTEGRATION! ☺

All of this is happening in The Permanent Now. The Permanent Now is The Stage on which ALL exists. Everything always existed, exists and will exist in this Moment – The Permanent Now.

After reading this simplistic chronology of the physical integration of part of this universe and the constant evolution and integration of The Permanent Now, does the importance of The Permanent Now come into focus?

THE LIVING LIFE

LIFE is The Permanent Now. Living in The Permanent Now is like playing the piano. Play every note to its fullest and give each note your full sincerity, attention and Watching Awareness. When another note comes, integrate into the next note. Stay Here, Now and do not stay with any note. Observe, hear and engage every note to its fullest and leave it where it is, back into NOthing-ness.

Now your internal sincerity and attention is within. Keep your internal sincerity and attention within and give some of your sincerity and attention to your outward five senses. Fully accept, engage and experience those stimuli. With simple repetition, this becomes less challenging.

LIFTING WEIGHTS AND RELATIVENESS

After Waking Up in The Permanent Now, I became Aware of the reality/realm of Relativeness at a broader and deeper level while lifting weights. After realizing this, I stopped counting repetitions while working out and I left the reality/realm of Relativeness.

I give active and internal nurturing of Watching Awareness from within for my internal state along with an intense attention on the lifting and dropping of weight. I am not focused on how much I lift or how many repetitions I complete. Only lifting.

I start with the bench press and over a two-week period, I work the bench press three times a week. In these six sessions, I increase the weight forty-eight percent, I use a spotter and the repetitions end up similar. Previously, I was not in The Permanent Now because I was counting. I stopped counting repetitions and living in illusory future consciousness and the weight increased forty-eight percent.

I was not Here, Now, while I was counting. I WAS WANTING to be there, then. When I counted one, two, three, etc., I was in a reality/realm of one-eighth, two-eighths, three-eighths, etc. the way to the end. I based my entire reality in the relative reality/realm of future consciousness.

My Awareness was focusing on future consciousness. I was not Here, Now. I was only one-eighth, two-eighths or three-eighths, etc. the way to where I wanted to be and it was somewhere in the illusory reality/realm of future consciousness. Relativeness.

I stopped counting, and I left the reality/realm of Relativeness. I continued this with the six major muscle groups and the increases in weight were thirty-six to seventy-six percent depending on the muscle group. Watch for relativeness. **Total fun!** ☺

You have boundless energy within **Y**ou. A hue of your most accurate Self is **Sheer Exuberance!**

DESCRIBING NOW

Describing Now is challenging for humans. Now holds very little interest to the human mind. Why? The Permanent Now has no conflict within it. The human mind knows how to deal with conflict. It is conflict. The human mind does not understand no conflict. It does not understand The Permanent Now.

To the human mind, Now is boredom and of no interest. It is the smallest amount of time, which is made for things to exist in. Humans are not accurately Aware of The Permanent Now. When you are, you will be Aware and on your knees laughing and happy-crying.

The Permanent Now is what is happening right in front of your face constantly, eternally and forever. The mind sees Now differently. The mind sees Now as a collection of things; people, places and events. It sees things here and when those things leave, change, etc. the mind sees Now as different from when the other stuff was here.

The Permanent Now is independent of Space, Time and Form. The Permanent Now allows Space, Time and Form to exist. The Permanent Now is constant. Things move in and out of The Stage called The Permanent Now. The Permanent Now does not change when things enter and leave.

There is only one Now, not an infinite amount of Nows, which are all changing based on people, places and events.

THE THREE REALMS

The Empirical, Cognitive/Mental and Spiritual Realms are

the three enveloping and increasing breadths and depths of Reality existing within yourself and this universe.

The Empirical Realm

The Empirical Realm is the realm of the things you can see, touch, hear, smell and taste or the realm of It.

Describing the Empirical Realm

If there are four apples, two oranges and a banana on a table and someone asks you and the other seven-and-a-half billion people on this planet how many apples there are on the table, everyone agrees there are four apples on the table. You can see, touch, smell and taste all the things on the table and come to the direct experience and realization there are four apples on the table. Because all seven-and-a-half billion people came up with the same results, everyone agrees accurate Reality has four apples on the table.

How do two people get the same results? When each person goes through the same process, they get the same results. In this example, everyone sees, tastes, smells or touches the different objects and comes to the same conclusion.

Therefore, if people do Step X, then Step Y and then Step Z, everyone comes up with the same conclusion.

The Cognitive/Mental Realm

The Cognitive/Mental Realm is the realm of things you can cognitively deduce in your brain. The Cognitive/Mental Realm is outside the Empirical Realm and envelopes it.

Describing the Cognitive/Mental Realm

Calculus are ideas and rules existing in the Mental Realm. You cannot quantify the infinitesimal and put it on a table and see it, taste it, touch it, smell it or hear it. Therefore, humans do not teach calculus until humans are Aware enough to be able to work in this area of the reality/realm of mental cognition.

How do two people get the same results? When each person goes through the same process, they get the same results. In this example, I leave the process to the mathematics teachers.

Therefore, if people do Step X, then Step Y and then Step Z, everyone comes up with the same conclusion.

The Spiritual Realm

The Spiritual Realm is the realm of Watching Awareness and The Permanent Now. The Spiritual Realm is the realm an individual can unveil after (s)he COMES BACK TO NOW and through repetition stays in The Permanent Now. The Spiritual Realm is outside the Empirical Realm and the Cognitive/Mental Realm and envelopes both.

The Spiritual Realm is the integration of both the Empirical and Cognitive/Mental Realms and the synergies that come with INTEGRATION.

Describing the Spiritual Realm

The Spiritual Realm is the realm of Watching Awareness. Watching Awareness unveils The Permanent Now. When you dis-identify with and let go of Time and all the illusions living in Time, you have a high potentiality to broaden and deepen your myopic Awareness. When you expand your myopic Awareness and go deeply into Awareness, you can come to the direct experience and realization of The Permanent Now, your most accurate Self and ALL.

How do two people get the same results? When each person goes through the same process, they get the same results. It is a letting go of self-identification with and attachment to Time and all the illusions living in Time.

The Permanent Now is where you can become Aware of and then Aware and then Aware of Awareness.

Therefore, if people do Step X, then Step Y and then Step Z, everyone comes up with the same conclusion.

Humans who have not grown up, matured, evolved and INTEGRATED beyond the Cognitive/Mental Realm almost always deny the Spiritual Realm. The mind holds on to the

Cognitive/Mental Realm for dear life. Because of the fear of change, most humans have difficulty accepting the next stage of INTEGRATION and evolution. Humans shy away from coming to their own direct experience and realization through the simple and observable process of Step X, then Step Y and then Step Z.

Here is one perspective on "the process" and it is not a process to unveil The Permanent Now, Awareness and your most accurate Self. This entire process is increasing the enveloping breadths and depths of your internal self-Awareness.

Step X – Use THE HERALDS OF NOW as archways and lighthouses to COME BACK TO NOW and with repetition stay Here, Now. Step Y – Come to the direct experience and realization of The Permanent Now. Step Z – Use The Permanent Now as the archway and lighthouse to unveil your most accurate Self, PURE AWARENESS-BLISS and THE SOURCE creat*ing* this universe.

Spirituality is full acceptance of The Permanent Now.

GRAPH NOW

Plotting a single moment on a graph shows a phenomenon. Plotting two moments on a graph shows a slope. Plotting three moments on a graph shows a trend. Plotting four moments on a graph shows a reality. If you are ever concerned Now is not always no more suffering, do the following. Take four moments of your life, while you live that moment and ask yourself if that moment is/has no suffering based on what that moment and only that specific moment is. Do not base the moment's no-more-suffering results with illusory past or future thought. Assess Now and come to the direct experience and realization there is never suffering Now. After you accurately assess Now, become more Aware there is no suffering when you live Here and in The Permanent Now. All form comes and goes. Do not resist this fact of the universe.

CONVERSATIONS IN THE NOW

When you stay Present, conversations do not unravel, become negative or have conflict within them. Stay Present. Be Watching Awareness. Listen. Present your point-of-view. Come to an amicable solution. **Y**ou create Reality.

IN BALANCE

You are creating this universe for all the "individual" forms of **Y**ou to live Here, Now and have experiences of integrative Change and Relationship. Form is in balance within The Permanent Now. Are you Aware of Form leaving Now and going there, then? Show me anything, which has been to the illusory past or future. Only the illusory self-identification with and attachment to the human mind does this. Space is in balance within The Permanent Now. Are you Aware of Space leaving Now and going there, then? No, you are not. Integrative change is in balance within The Permanent Now. Only self-identification with and attachment to the human mind goes there, then.

THE ROCK AND THE CREEK

While walking across some rocks in a creek, a rock shifted below me. Before Waking Up, I would assume, a future-based mental activity, I was going to fall and I would have compensated. The assumption and compensation would have most likely made me fall into the creek. Previously, I thought I would fall and I would create what I thought.

With a smile on my face, I stayed Present, did not assume anything, kept my balance and kept walking across the creek. You always have your balance in The Permanent Now. Live in The Permanent Now and do not force things. Most events come to pass with pleasantness and without the illusory individual me/ego trying to control the event, people or outcome to get what the illusory individual me/ego feels it needs to finally find Happiness and Connection.

The Permanent Now, where Time is not.

REALITY AND PHILOSOPHY

"There is only one really serious philosophical question, and that is suicide." – Albert Camus

Mr. Camus' statement is not as accurate as it could be. A more accurate statement is, "There is only one sincere philosophical question, and that is whether to live in Reality, The Permanent Now." – FRITZ

Merriam-Webster's online dictionary defines philosophy as:
: the study of ideas about knowledge, truth, the nature and meaning of life, etc. – The meaning of LIFE is Now.
: a particular set of ideas about knowledge, truth, the nature and meaning of life, etc. – You come to this direct experience and realization in The Permanent Now.
: a set of ideas about how to do something or how to live – You only live in The Permanent Now.

The only way you will accurately accomplish any of the above is to live in the Here and The Permanent Now. Now is Reality. The Permanent Now is without Time. Why are you trying to escape something you cannot get out of? The Permanent Now is All There Is.

LIVE SIMPLY AND SIMPLY LIVE

People who live simply and simply live can be much less connected to self-identification with and attachment to Time and all the illusions living in Time than people who live complexly and complexly live. How? Lessen the spell of myopic physical and mental materialism. Materialism hypnotizes humans.

TIME DOES NOT AFFECT REALITY

The illusory past and future do not affect The Permanent Now. They never have and they never will. Only The Permanent Now exists. THERE ARE NO PROBLEMS NOW. Go do what you want in this life. Unveil your most accurate Self and live your most accurate life.

FEEL LOST?

You are always where you are supposed to be, right Here and in The Permanent Now. COME BACK TO NOW and with repetition unveil The Permanent Now.

ETERNALISM AND PRESENTISM

TIME does not exist. Integrative change in The Permanent Now most definitely exists.

Exchange TIME with "Integrative Change in The Permanent Now" and watch how your view of Reality changes.

The Arrow of Time is INTEGRATION. We all know this universe does not "un-integrate." Things do not go back the way they were, Mr. Dumpty.

Take aspects of Eternalism and Presentism and integrate them and you can potentially see Reality, The Permanent Now.

NOTE

Under the current and dynamic seven, large-plate-tectonic geographic relationship.

The Permanent Now
is all there was, is and all
there ever will be

only way to learn

through direct realization

The Permanent Now

QUESTIONS

WHO AM I?

Then…

An excellent son, brother, friend

An excellent business development executive

A positive person

NOW…

A question is looking for an answer. More accurately, a thing is looking for Happiness and Connection. The understanding of the answer is not the outcome. It is the beginning of unveiling Watching Awareness.

If I'm already enlightened, why do I not feel different?
Your self-identification with and attachment to Time and all the illusions living in Time masks and covers Awareness, The Permanent Now and your most accurate Self.

A major misconception humans have is spiritual Awakening brings Happiness. Happiness is the other side of the spectrum to Sadness and Suffering – The Illusion of Duality. Happiness is another thought the mind has for the opposite of Suffering. Both are illusory. Live as Watching Awareness and come to the direct experience and realization there is a lot more to accurate Reality than what the human mind calls Happiness and its perceived opposite, Sadness.

There is an infinite breadth and depth to accurate Joy, Stillness, Love, Serenity and Connection in The Permanent Now. Accurate Joy, Stillness, Love, Serenity and Connection are real and greatly differ from what the mind labels Happiness.

Where can I find accurate and sustaining Joy, Peace, Love, Serenity and Connection?

The Permanent Now. The human mind thinks it can find Joy, Stillness, Love, Serenity and Connection in the things it creates, self-identifies with and attaches to. It cannot. Accurate Joy, Stillness, Love, Serenity and Connection and no more suffering are innate to Awareness, The Permanent Now and your most accurate Self. They are not things to grasp for and hold on to during the perceived tumultuous events of life.

How do I come to the direct experience and realization of something?

Watch. Watch everything on the outside and watch everything on the inside; your thoughts, feelings, emotions, etc. You must watch.

If this whole universe is manifested heaven, why are there bad people committing atrocities?

When you resist The Permanent Now, you turn away from, cover up and blind yourself to manifested heaven and land in a perceived and an illusory-only hell. Three major illusions of this illusory-only hell are The Illusion of Separation, Relativeness and Time. Myopically believing in, self-identifying with and attaching to these three illusory-only foundational pillars prop-up this illusory-only hell. These illusions are the source of and the catalysts for all the behaviors humans perpetrate on themselves, each other, other species and this planet*.

The Illusion of Separation also known as, "I'm a different thing than that thing over there and I'm a separate and an alone being in this universe, etc....," makes humans believe they are doing these atrocities on someone other than another version of their most accurate Self.

Humans' constant, petty and immature game of Relativeness also known as, "I'm better than you, therefore, I can do this, that and the other thing to you," makes humans experience the intoxicating comfort of committing these atrocities.

The Illusion of Time allows humans to give and accept reasons and excuses for present events to leverage the atrocities in The Permanent Now so they can barter for, negotiate against and reconcile with those actions in an illusory "better future."

If the past and future never existed, are you telling me dinosaurs did not exist?

Dinosaurs most definitely existed.

They existed in the less integrated Permanent Now. Dinosaurs did not live "in the past." They lived on the Stage of The Permanent Now. The thing you call the past never existed. Only less integrated versions of The Permanent Now existed. **THIS IS NOT WORDSMITHING.** When you come to this direct experience and realization your awakening is beginning.

The past and future only exist in the illusory reality/realm of mental cognition and conceptualization.

When you come to the direct experience and realization, the past and future are illusory and you unveil The Permanent Now, which has in it less integrated versions of The Permanent Now and more integrated versions of The

Permanent Now, your awakening and Self-realization are very close. ☺

All I need to do is watch?

If all I have "to do" is watch, won't this make me starve and die because I am not doing anything?

The question has presuppositions. No. **Y**ou never die. Watch. Go about your day and watch everything. There is no real individual you. The illusory individual you is not doing anything other than resisting The Permanent Now. Read The Flow paragraph again.

Watch. Go about your day. Watch everything. Release your myopic obsession with Fear and the desire to control this universe and watch the resistance, conflict and suffering end and unveil manifested heaven, PURE AWARENESS-BLISS and your most accurate Self.

When you let go of Fear, you let go of Control. When you fully let go of both illusions, you can begin your awakening.

If spiritual enlightenment is our natural state of existence, why are there so few Awakens/living buddhas around?

Humans do not want to look inside and deal with any of their internal issues.

"The most terrifying thing is to accept oneself completely."
– Carl Jung

Humans think The Shadow is real and therefore choose not to grow up and face their own internal issues, demons and monsters.

Quite ironically, the turning away from your internal issues, demons and monsters is exactly the catalyst for believing and perceiving The Shadow is real.

Watch, stare down and face your Shadow and it vanishes into Joy. Literally.

NOTE

After you Awaken, you come to the direct experience and realization there are only different versions of your most accurate Self. <u>You cannot blame anyone else</u>*[2]. There is only **You**.

NOTE2

Your most accurate Self <u>is not</u> a tyrannical, autocratic and monarchical leader*[3]. As an engaged, sincere and conscientious citizen of any balanced, healthy and mature society, you adhere to and believe in democratic rule, correct? Why would your most accurate Self be a tyrannical, autocratic and monarchical leader? No superiority. No Relativeness.

NOTE3

Most western religions have a tyrannical, autocratic and monarchical leader/god*4. In the West, this is based on Cyrus the Great, circa 600 B.C.E.

NOTE4

After you chisel away all the layers of eastern religions like Hinduism, Buddhism, Taoism, Zen, etc., you realize these religions are more accurately styles and ways of living an accurate life and less accurately belief systems known as Religion.

Western religions are belief systems. You get into heaven with right-belief not with right-doing. Sin is alleviated with right-belief, not right-doing. Religions are about mental cognition and **NOT** about direct experience and realization. Religious leaders hypnotize humans and are the hypnotizers of humanity.

questions are looking
for answers and connection
The Permanent Now

what's next in this life

laughter, Joy, Stillness and Love

The Permanent Now

WHAT IS NEXT

PURE AWARENESS-BLISS

Then…

God was mean, vengeful and petty

God was found after thoughts were preached, taught and learned

God was not for me

NOW…

Awareness is all there is

Awareness has awakened within

You are PURE AWARENESS-BLISS

Are you Aware of the amount of TIME and suffering you bring into your life and EXISTENCE? It Is What It Is. Are you ready to dis-identify with and give up attachment to time-consciousness, thought-consciousness and resistance to The Permanent Now? **You can Wake Up**. Awakening is not hard, difficult and certainly not impossible. Develop your ability to apply sincerity and attention to The Permanent Now. Sincerity and attention for humans is undervalued, underappreciated and way underdeveloped. You can do this!

Any challenge to Awakening lies in the understanding being an Awaken or a buddha is your natural state of balance and Being. Awakening is an integrating, an unfolding and an unveiling. It is simple, easy and not automatic for the individual. Repetition of consistent and internal nurturing of Watching Awareness from within for one's internal state is what should be given sincerity and attention. Small steps. **Continuously with a smile. Do not stop. Do not expect.**

THE SHADOW AND ITS INTERACTIONS

The Shadow is the part of the psyche which has no Light shining on it. **Awareness is The Light.** The Shadow is the resistance to The Permanent Now and all your unresolved past and future issues you bury in the deep recesses of your psyche. The Shadow is Time and the illusory reality/realm of past and future consciousness.

Come to the direct experience and realization of the resistance you have for aspects of your inner self, lower this resistance to those aspects of your inner self by Watching and then hug The Shadow.

Stare down your demons. Peer directly into the demon's existence. Figuratively, press your forehead and nose firmly against your demon's forehead and nose. **Press forward with a smirk.** Peer into that demon's existence and watch it dissolve into Joy. **Literally.**

Come to the direct experience and realization the demon was always illusory and The Permanent Now is. ☺!

All your external life issues you have are outward projections of your unresolved internal issues. You project your Shadow out into the world and therefore, never lower that resistance nor hug that resistance, your Shadow.

When you lower resistance to The Shadow you release its substantiality and importance and unveil its illusoriness. When you resist The Shadow, you give The Shadow substance, compulsion and importance. Crazy cyclical, huh?

The only way to let resistance out of your life is to fully accept the resistance and conflict. This might sound crazy. I am Aware. ☺ Lightness of Being is awesome.

"What you resist, persists." – Carl Jung

Do not fight the fighter. Fully accept the mental fighter and unveil the fighter's illusoriness. Do not resist your unresolved issues. Fully accept unresolved issues and the unresolved issues literally turn into Joy and then vanish. As you keep COMING BACK TO NOW, these vanishings increase in frequency. From the point-of-view of the human mind, this advice is crazy. Crazy is something out of the norm. Out of the norm is the path you are trying to unveil, correct? The norm got you Here, correct? Read the definition of Insanity, right now. Read the car driving on ice paragraph, right now.

The human mind lives in a reality/realm of competition, fighting, resistance, conflict and suffering. The human mind knows nothing about acceptance without condition. Full acceptance has no conditions. **Be noble and brave.**

The pain you associate with The Shadow is not real. I am Aware you think the pain is real. By Watching, push through, past and out of the illusory pain and come to the direct experience and realization the pain keeping you in your comfort zones is not real. The pain you associate with The Shadow is not real.

How can an illusion create anything REAL?

Continuously with a smile. Do not stop. Do not expect.

Sleep tight in your bed tonight
All is right and bright

Be a knight tonight
There is no fright, spite or slight

Reread the first three sentences of Chapter Four, right now. How can anyone else stare down your internal issues, demons and monsters for you? Do not follow anyone other than yourself. Obviously, you should follow accurate guidance. ☺

THINKING, BELIEVING, KNOWING, ETC.

Thinking, believing and knowing are increasing levels of maturity of thought. You are becoming increasingly more self-identified with and attached to thought. Humans give their authority over and identity up to things and therefore You get lost in those things. If you believe you are things, trapped by those things and controlled by those things, you choose a delusional reality controlled by resistance, conflict and suffering and created by self-identification with and attachment to Time and all the illusions living in Time.

However, if you expand your breadths and depths of Awareness, by not self-identifying with and attaching to Time and all the illusions living in Time and therefore do not self-identify with and give attachment to Space, Time and Form and make a conscious inward decision to let go of the illusory reality/realm of past and future consciousness, you will come to the direct experience and realization of; Awareness, NOthing, PURE AWARENESS-

BLISS and your most accurate Self. You will not mentally suffer anymore and you will understand how to live in The Permanent Now. The only place that ever exists.

TURNING AWAY

If you turn away from the signposts in The Permanent Now and other places, your suffering continues. You bought your suffering with the price of apathy.

This is fine. This is your choice. Humans have been turning away from What Is for the entire history of the human species. If this is the mentality you hold, be Aware of your choice and this mentality and move on. The mentality to turn away from What Is, is the same mentality another group of humans possessed when Galileo Galilei showed them Jupiter and her moons with a telescope. Those humans turned away from What Is. They also locked Galileo away for showing them Reality. The mind becomes scared when it sees Reality. You laugh and happy-cry when you see Reality.

Turning your mental back on What Is does not change Reality. Jupiter and her moons still revolve around the Sun. The Permanent Now is all there is. ☺ Turning away from What Is keeps the turner in the darkness of TIME, unconsciousness and mental suffering. What label do humans use to describe someone unAware of Reality? Insane.

CHANGE

Change is inevitable in this universe. This universe is change. Not accepting the most fundamental structure of this universe is insanity and creates resistance. This resistance creates Time, conflict and suffering. You resist the constant and positive one-way evolution of this universe, integrative change, and this resistance to The Flow of this universe lands you in a perceived and illusory-only hell. Then you spend an entire lifetime trying to get out of a perceived and illusory-only hell that does not exist! Then, at your perceived and illusory-only individual life's illusory end, the illusion you self-identify with and attach to rages against the end of the light. Very dramatic. Very unnecessary*. Accept change wholeheartedly. There is no reason to fear change. **Be noble and brave.**

TAKING RESPONSIBILITY

If you are an older reader and you watch questions like this pass through your Awareness, "If this universe is manifested heaven, how come my life ended up this way, that way or the other way?", you need to unveil the resistance you gave certain parts of your life when your most accurate Self gave you a gift. Come to the direct experience and realization of those moments of resistance.

All humans self-identify with and attach Fear and Separation to this experience called "my life." Because of your fear and apprehension toward stepping out of your comfort zone and fully living life, you resisted gifts this universe gave you and chose not to accept those gifts based on the illusory perception the universe is not providing a friendly relationship with you and/or you feel you are not worthy of gifts.

Stop resisting The Permanent Now and unveil the innate friendship you have with this universe.

NOTE

You Wake Up from the dream you and I call this universe. You Wake Up to REAL LIFE.

want enlightenment
constantly get with What Is
you're already Home

resisting Heaven
creates the search for pleasure
breathe deep and Watching

ANALOGIES

THE MOTH

The moth draws its sincerity and attention to flame and is consumed within that union. The human species draws its sincerity and attention to TIME and is consumed within that union. A buddha's sincerity and attention is The Permanent Now.

THE LEAF

Watch a leaf float down the creek. Should the leaf go left or right around a boulder in the creek? What cares where the leaf goes? No matter what side of the boulder the leaf goes, it is the same creek and the same water. Eventually, the leaf ends up at the same place. Does the leaf need to get on the left side of the boulder and therefore get to the end of the creek quicker? Will going on the boulder's left side make the leaf a better leaf than if the leaf went on the boulder's the right side? Will the other leaves in the creek look at this leaf in dismay if this leaf goes around the boulder's left side? Will the other leaves look at this leaf with awe if this leaf goes around the boulder's right side? ☺ Find the thing inside wanting control over the leaf's path?

The Farmer

Once upon a time, a farmer enters her vast, empty and fertile field to plant her beautiful flowers, seeds and shade-bearing trees. If her pockets are not empty when she bends down to plant the seeds, unknowingly her pockets will release undesirable weeds into her fertile soil. The weeds she is unAware of will grow around her knowingly planted seeds. The unknowingly planted weeds grow quickly and choke out her seeds. The weeds cause damage, mayhem and suffering to her field. She could look at the field in disgust and remorse; never realizing just under the top layer of weeds is a rich, fertile and wondrous field waiting to Be. The farmer does not have to live this way.

A farmer enters her vast, empty and fertile field to plant her beautiful flowers, seeds and shade-bearing trees. Because her pockets are actively, carefully and attentively checked for their emptiness when she bends down to plant the seeds she has brought to her field, she has a lush and active field which bears all the manifestations of her doings. While reaping the aesthetic enjoyments of her flowers, nourishing herself with fruit and enjoying the shade of her trees, she actively, carefully and attentively tends to any weeds, popping up from time to time. Her field flourishes. The farmer looks at her field with appreciation and enjoys a life of Peace while actively Aware of what she did not do.

The Teeter Totter

The more you self-identify with and attach to Time and all the illusions living in Time the more perceived mental weight each thought has.

You are standing on and in the middle of a teeter-totter. You look to your left and you are Aware of all the thoughts about your past. You look to your right and you are Aware all the thoughts about your future.

When you myopically focus on the illusory reality/realm past or future consciousness, you move on the teeter-totter in an outward direction. The weight of those thoughts pulls you from the middle of the teeter-totter, the place of balance, The Permanent Now, toward the illusory reality/realm of past and future consciousness.

When your Watching Awareness myopically focusses on thought "about the past," you self-identify with and attach to the illusory past consciousness. When your Watching Awareness myopically focusses on thought "about the future," you self-identify with and attach to the illusory future consciousness.

The human mind wants peace. When it cannot find peace in the illusory past, it searches in the illusory future and vice versa. This searching creates attachment and causes a lot of temporal mental movement back and forth. Self-identification with and attachment to the illusory reality/realm of past and future consciousness and mental temporal movement in Time is resistance, conflict and suffering.

From the mind's perspective, finding peace is like trying to walk a camel through the eye of a needle. The mind says, "I'm not sure how I will do this, but (conflict) I have hope (thought) tomorrow (future) will be a better day (the illusory past and future consciousness).

Come to the direct experience and realization of accurate Peace and Connection, in The Permanent Now, and stay in the middle of the teeter-totter and unveil Stillness. **Y**ou are already Here, Now. Self-identification with and attachment to Time and all the illusions living in Time are not.

Being Here, Now is easier than falling over and hitting the ground. **Y**ou do not have to do anything.

SUTRAS

Resting

Then…

Was for tired people

Was for Sunday

NOW…

I rest and Be

What You Resist, Persists

Jamming a stick into a riverbed creates resistance and turmoil in the water's flow. If you spend energy keeping the stick jammed in the riverbed, will the stick ever stop resisting the water's flow?

If you allow the stick to stop resisting the water and let the stick float on top of the water, will you see turmoil, resistance and conflict between the water's flow and the stick? Will there be any turmoil within the relationship between the stick and the river?

WHAT YOU FULLY ACCEPT GOES AWAY

Resistance and conflict exist in relationship with other resistance and conflict. Resistance does not live in The Permanent Now. Resistance and conflict need, in mountain climbing lingo, purchase or a point of leverage. Resistance and conflict need a foothold to gain purchase and leverage for the next thing coming up, which is more resistance and conflict. Crazy cyclical, huh?

When there is no place for leverage or resistance, there is no way for resistance to breed conflict and to leverage itself against a perceived other thing. Fully accept what has already happened while being in the Now and unveil Watching Awareness.

Do not allow resistance and conflict to grab a foothold and obtain purchase or a place of leverage in your life. Resistance and conflict cannot survive without another foothold for it to leverage against, which is judgment and self-identification with and attachment to the illusory reality/realm of past and future consciousness.

MORE SIGNPOSTS

CONVERSATIONS AMONGST TWO FRIENDS

#1

Friend1 – I need your help with a philosophy paper.

Friend2 – Cool.

Friend1 – What's the difference between Reality and religion?

Friend2 – Religion promises you the truth **if** you follow and accept their thoughts and belief system. Buddhas talk about Waking Up and living in The Permanent Now. We provide guidance. Everything else takes care of itself.

Friend1 – Got it. Thanks. What about the truth?

Friend2 – You're welcome. Everything's true and false.

Friend1 – Huh?

Friend2 – Reality's about Accuracy not the truthness and falseness of the relative absoluteness of a very temporal thing labeled thought.

#2

Friend1 – Where does a first-day seeker say her sincerity and attention lie?

Friend2 – Watching begins from within.

Friend1 – Where does a second-day seeker say his sincerity and attention lie?

Friend2 – Listening begins from within.

Friend1 – Where does a third-day seeker say her sincerity and attention lie?

Friend2 – Seeing begins from within.

Friend1 – Where does a fourth-day seeker say his sincerity and attention lie?

Friend2 – Tasting begins from within.

Friend1 – Where does a fifth-day seeker say her sincerity and attention lie?

Friend2 – Smelling begins from within.

Friend1 – Where does a sixth-day seeker say his sincerity and attention lie?

Friend2 – Touching begins from within.

Friend1 – What does a buddha say?

Friend2 – Not much. ☺

#3

Friend1 – What did you say about life? "It's all good?"

Friend2 – It's always all good.

Friend1 – How does this help me?

Friend2 – If you were ABSOLUTELY Aware everything is always good, how would you change your engagement with yourself, others, your life and this universe?
Friend1 – Huh?
Friend2 – Your fear of LIFE and the desire to have control over LIFE would dissolve and your engagement with LIFE would increase exponentially.

#4
Friend1 – What was that riddle you were talking about?
Friend2 – What's the thing you cannot escape and cannot attain?
Friend1 – I have no idea.
Friend2 – Your most accurate Self.

#5
Friend1 – Why don't you ever complain about anything?
Friend2 – I hang out in the only place there is.
Friend1 – Oh yeah, what bar is that?
Friend2 – It's not a bar. It's The Permanent Now.
Friend1 – Really!? I'm with you now and I complain.
Friend2 – Is that so?
Friend1 – How can this stuff help me make more money so I can get more stuff and be better?
Friend2 – Read The Permanent Now and tell me if you still live in the same place I do.

#6

Friend1 – When you are in The Permanent Now, is there ever a problem?

Friend2 – No.

Friend1 – Can you help me understand why I don't live in The Permanent Now?

Friend2 – You choose to experience Time and Suffering.

Friend1 – That's mean.

Friend2 – What thing is labeling it mean? **Watch.**

#7

Friend1 – Why do you just sit around and smile? Go do something!

Friend2 – There's nothing left to do. ☺

"Your own Self-realization is the greatest service
you can render the world."

Ramana Maharshi

ABOUT THE AUTHOR

Fritz grew up in Colorado, Iowa and Texas.

Fritz lives in The Permanent Now and is an Awaken – a living buddha.

At fifteen, Fritz began searching for a way out of suffering and at thirty-eight, Fritz literally Woke Up in The Permanent Now, spiritually Awakened and came to the direct experience and realization that self-identification with and attachment to Time and all the illusions living in Time is illusory.

Fritz's writings provide shrewd and exceptionally accurate guidance to spiritual Awakening and enlightenment, crafted by a living buddha.

Fritz's brevity, sincerity and attention deliver concise and easy to read writings on spiritual Awakening and enlightenment.

After awakening, Fritz wrote The Permanent Now and Haiku to The Permanent Now – Volumes One, Two, Three, Four, Five, Six, Seven and Eight, which provide exceptionally accurate guidance to spiritual Awakening and enlightenment.

Use Fritz's writings as guidance to spiritual Awakening and enlightenment and help you literally Wake Up and unveil your most accurate Self and live your most accurate life in accurate Reality, The Permanent Now.

WWW.THEPERMANENTNOW.COM

HERE'S THE DEAL

There is only **The Permanent Now**. THERE ARE NO PROBLEMS NOW. You do not have to leave Now and go there, then for any reason, especially to solve a problem, which does not exist Now. You think you must go there, then because you live in Time and the illusory reality/realm of past and future consciousness.

Your most accurate Self is dreaming this universe. **The Permanent Now** only has different breadths and depths of PURE AWARENESS-BLISS. JOY. STILLNESS. LOVE.

You cannot change who **Y**ou are. **Y**ou are the field of Watching Awareness. You can INTEGRATE more of who **Y**ou are into what you think you are and therefore increase your potentiality to Awaken and unveil through your direct experience and realization your most accurate Self is ALL.

You are not a separate being trying to secure the approval of any god to get into any heaven. You are not a separate being trying to figure out how to fit into this random, mindless and machine-like universe, which keeps chugging along with or without you. These are dogmas.

Actively lower resistance to aspects of your inner self and accept those aspects of your inner self. Move through, past and out of the illusory reality/realm of past and future consciousness and Wake Up in **The Permanent Now**.

Use THE HERALDS OF NOW as archways and lighthouses to COME BACK TO NOW and with repetition stay Here, Now and unveil **The Permanent Now**. Use **The Permanent Now** as the archway and lighthouse to unveil your most accurate Self, PURE AWARENESS-BLISS - THE SOURCE CREATING THIS UNIVERSE.

Small steps. Continuously with a smile. **Do not stop. Do not expect.** Unveil your most accurate Self and live your most accurate life. All the best.

Made in the USA
Las Vegas, NV
05 October 2021